What Others Are Saying about *Zero to One Million*

Forgive Ryan Allis for being so young. Forgive him for imparting time-less wisdom based upon his own real-life experience as an entrepre-neurial superstar. The kid just can't help it. He has made a million-dollar dream come true and he shares how he did it in this roller-coaster-of-a-read book. Your banker will love you for reading it.

—*Jay Conrad Levinson, The Father of Guerrilla Marketing,*
Author, Guerrilla Marketing *series of books*

Ryan Allis shares an intriguing story of business success that has few parallels. I know of no other person so young who has demonstrated this level of achievement in business. Young people need individuals like Ryan to look up to and emulate as they work to accomplish their own personal and business goals.

—*David S. Chernow, President and CEO,*
Junior Achievement Worldwide

Zero to One Million is going to inspire a new generation of aspiring entrepreneurs. If you are thinking about starting a company or own one now, this is the book for you.

—*Jeff Reid, Executive Director,*
Center for Entrepreneurship, UNC—Chapel Hill

Ryan writes this book as he is creating his multi-million-dollar com-pany. His viewpoints are those of someone in the midst of the strug-gles and triumphs that every successful "entrepreneur in the making" goes through. Ryan has written one of the best business start-up and growth books that I have ever read. This book is written in a way that seems like your best friend has just found his success and wants to help you achieve that same success. For me, this book was one I just could not put down. It is a very easy and enjoyable read. I rec-ommend *Zero to One Million* as an inspirational read to any young person with a dream of one day starting his or her own company.

—*Joshua A. Mitchell, CEO of Riakt Studios*

Zero to One Million gives a lot of insight into the world of business. I enjoined the recap of history. Ryan is right in his assertion that not all are given equal standing in the world. This is a sad fact of life but also a great factor in why humanity strives to succeed. His understanding of entrepreneurship and economics is amazing. Through his book, he has drastically moved my mindset, from isolationism to that of open markets. Freedom and wealth will flow best through open gates.

—*Tiana Laurence, Aspen, Colorado*

Zero To One Million provides good instruction [on] how to lay a foundation for a successful company. Ryan explains how he got his foundation of being an entrepreneur and gives pointers on how to become a successful entrepreneur. He does all of this while giving a background on how entrepreneurship affects each of us individually and why it is important for our country to continue to think entrepreneurially. This book is a gem for young aspiring entrepreneurs like myself and to others who feel they may need help with advancing the sales of their business.

—*Jason Robertson, North Carolina*

Ryan Allis has written a book that acts as an inspiration for business people all over the world. At an age where most people are developing a sense of business savvy, he has mastered it and shares his knowledge with the masses. I read this book with a highlighter in hand to ensure that I would not miss out on the underlying points of importance. He proves that the dream of entrepreneurship can be a reality for anyone, and I look forward to his insight in books to come.

—*Nicholas Lombardi, Wallingford, Connecticut*

Ryan Allis gives a captivating account of his experience as an entrepreneur. Most books on entrepreneurship are either too exciting or too focused on the hard work. This one presents entrepreneurship as a field of endeavor that I liken to gardening: you have to plant correctly, water correctly, fertilize correctly, and the business will grow. Entrepreneurship is the business of patience, not enthusiasm, not money, not motivation, not hope, not determination nor courage. While all these play their part, patience seems to be the critical ingredient that most people don't have to succeed. If you keep doing the right things, your business will grow to one million dollars in sales.

—*Martin Messier, Brazil*

For those who are ready, this book can be your launching pad. I found it enlightening and incredibly empowering. Ryan allows his passion to fully shine through and after reading *Zero to One Million* I have been inspired to find mine in life. I've always wanted to make a difference in our world, and Ryan beautifully articulates how that time is now. He truly grasps how our world is rapidly changing and reveals that it is an emerging minority of young entrepreneurs that will make this change in the coming years. Don't wait . . . have a bias toward action and take control of your life now!

—*Greg Mueller, Durham, North Carolina*

This book is not a get rich quick guide; it is a handbook that you will continue to use as a reference and it is a book that will instill important business concepts. One of the most important aspects of being an entrepreneur is confidence. As I read this book, I found myself more and more confident in the goals that I had set for myself, and the business that my partners and I were in the process of starting. Ryan clearly outlines the steps to starting a business, and provides a very informative section devoted to search engine optimization. This book should be read by anyone who has a desire to start a business, and has a pro-active attitude towards life. It is great to know that someone of Ryan's age could be so business-savvy, self-disciplined, and biased towards action . . . that is empowering.

—*Jacob Bohall, Hilton Head, South Carolina*

I love *Zero to One Million*—not like—LOVE! You've inspired me! My goals, mission and creed are framed and on the wall. I love the MAR Model for evaluating business ideas. You manage to get all this stuff that I've known about for years and somehow get me to act on it, be excited about it, and get results! I just keep raving about it to people. I most often say, "One of the endorsements on the book says 'Ryan is the next Robert Kiyosaki,' and they're absolutely right." Ryan's writing gets me into action. It took me a few weeks (instead of a day) to read the book because I kept *doing* what he was talking about. I came away from each chapter not only having my thoughts cleared, but with an action plan and an elevated spirit, fire in my heart, wind at my heels, ready to get on with it.

—*Jade Barclay, Queensland, Australia*

Zero to One Million was awesome. I spent the better part of the first night I received it (when I was supposed to be sleeping) reading it. I was doing the old flashlight under the covers trick since I had to be up at 6:00 the next morning for school, and Mom would have sent me to bed had she known. No matter—I felt it was good preparation for me becoming an entrepreneur. The book has made a difference in one life. All books I had read previously (Robert Kiyosaki, Robert Allen), while containing good information, had left me still a little confused as to where I was going. After reading this book, there was no doubt in my mind. I am going to be an entrepreneur—and a successful one. I really liked the book's down-to-earth style with practical examples. Thanks a million (pun intended).

—*Greg, British Columbia, Canada*

After reading *Zero to One Million* and implementing the strategies and techniques in Mr. Allis's book, my business revenue has almost tripled in a short four-month time. I am the CEO of a nutraceutical corporation and interact with CEOs from companies in the USA and internationally. I can honestly say I have tried multiple methods and hired multiple marketing and management teams in the past, spending hundreds of thousands of dollars with little to no results. I have also read multiple books on subjects of personal and business development including Stephen Covey, Richard Gerber, Anthony Robbins, Louise Hay, Dale Carnegie and more. *Zero to One Million* covers the beginner to advanced stages it takes to become successful and financially secure. I would recommend this book to all entrepreneurs and successful business men and women.

—*Dr. Edward F. Group, Houston, Texas*

This book contains a wealth of information and inspiration. Ryan is the next Robert Kiyosaki.

—*Michael Simmons, author,* The Student Success Manifesto

I like *Zero to One Million* a lot. I like the style. It is easy to read—even for me. You have done a great job of picking up on the copy writing nuances that make a piece impossible to put down.

—*Robert Ryan, Petagonia*

I think one of the best ways to learn is by example and that is what is so beautiful about *Zero to One Million*. I believe that the way to becoming successful in life is to study those who are. In this book not only does Ryan teach you so much about the history of economics and business, but he shares every step of how he got to where he is today.

—*Jenna Horshaver*

ZERO
TO ONE
MILLION

ZERO
TO ONE
MILLION

HOW I BUILT A COMPANY TO
$1 MILLION IN SALES...
AND HOW YOU CAN, TOO

RYAN P. ALLIS

New York Chicago San Francisco Lisbon London Madrid Mexico City
Milan New Delhi San Juan Seoul Singapore Sydney Toronto

The *McGraw·Hill* Companies

3 4 5 6 7 8 9 0   FGR/FGR   0 9 8

ISBN: 978-0-07-149666-7
MH ID: 0-07-149666-1

Library of Congress Cataloging-in-Publication Data

Allis, Ryan P. M.
  Zero to one million : how I built a company to $1 million in sales . . . and how you can, too / by Ryan P. M. Allis.
    p. cm.
  ISBN 0-07-149666-1 (alk. paper)
  1. New business enterprises. 2. Entrepreneurship. 3. Success in business. I. Title.

HD62.5.A462 2008
658.1'1—dc22   2007044520

This book is printed on acid-free paper.

CONTENTS

APPENDIXES

ACKNOWLEDGMENTS

Building a company to a million dollars in sales cannot be done alone. This book is dedicated to my business partner, Aaron Houghton, and the truly rock-star team we have at iContact. I wish also to thank the following family members, friends, colleagues, and institutions that have made this book possible.

- Donya Dickerson
- Rick Broadhead
- Andrew Allis, Sr.
- Pauline Middleton Allis
- Andrew Allis, Jr.
- Erin Mulfinger
- Marti Kiely
- Steve Kiely
- Aaron Houghton
- David Roth
- David Rasch
- Brandon Milford
- Tim Oakley
- Chuck Hester
- Robert Plumley
- Amber Neill
- Matt Allen
- Cindy Hays
- Michelle Tabares
- Alan Cox
- Geoff Caitlin
- Alan Underwood

- Erik Severinghaus
- Wes Garrison
- Malcolm Young
- Russ Jones
- Jeff Staub
- Carter Griffin
- Conor Mullett
- Monica Doss
- Evelyn Williams
- Michael Simmons
- Michael McNyne
- Jeff Reid
- Robert Fletcher
- Kristina Hager
- Alex Hardy
- Merrill Mason
- Buck Goldstein
- Barry Roberts
- Colin Wahl
- Christy Shaffer
- Dave Rizzo
- Merrette Moore
- Randy Myer
- Alston Gardner
- Jud Bowman
- Scot Wingo
- Michael Doernberg
- Kevin Fitzgerald
- Carolina Entrepreneurship Club
- Collegiate Entrepreneurs' Organization
- The Kauffman Foundation
- The State of North Carolina
- UNC Center for Entrepreneurship
- UNC Kenan-Flagler Business School
- The Entire iContact Family

FOREWORD

by Michael Simmons

Zero to One Million is about expanding access to entrepreneurial opportunity, one of the key principles the United States was founded upon. It's about spreading the knowledge of how to build a successful venture. *Zero to One Million* is a guide for aspiring and current entrepreneurs that explains, step-by-step, how to build a company to $1 million in sales. The book provides an unprecedented level of access and insight into an actual multi-million-dollar company. Ryan's experience building iContact to over $10 million in annual sales and over 80 employees gives the book depth and excitement.

Ryan shares how and why every element worked and examines every process, every system, every technique, and every strategy in a manner that can be applied to any business, whether you have just a fledging idea, a mature local company, or a high-potential start-up. This book shows how anyone can build a million-dollar company, or if already there, expand sales even further.

This book is organized into three parts. In Part One Ryan tells his captivating story. It narrates how he went from being an 11-year-old living on a small island off the west coast of Florida to a marketing consultant for a company in the health products industry at age 17 that went from zero to $1 million in sales in just over a year, to co-founding an investor-backed software start-up at age 18, to being CEO of a company with over $10 million in annual sales by age 23.

Part Two provides a 10-step process for building a company from the ground to $1 million in sales. This section covers how the system of entrepreneurship works and how to find your core motivation, determine what to sell, evaluate opportunities, write a business plan, obtain funding, develop a product, build your marketing and sales strategies, build your team, become a manager, and build systems. These chapters will take you from the point of not being sure what to sell up to the point where you are ready to launch and expand. The essential due diligence, planning, and infrastructure-building processes are detailed with a step-by-step guide that can be applied to any type of start-up or small business.

Step 7 covers marketing and sales strategy. Many aspiring entrepreneurs create an innovative product, do their market research, raise the money, incorporate their company, build the infrastructure, and bring on great people, but fail to get sales going. This section details how to complete market research, gain competitive intelligence, execute marketing campaigns, build customer relationships, and grow online sales. The Web marketing section provides a guide to creating your Web site, getting to the top of the major search engines, building links, leveraging e-mail marketing, and launching a partner program.

Once you have succeeded in executing your marketing plan, your company will be entering a period of growth. How you manage that growth and how you adapt to these changes will determine whether you can sustain that growth and cross the proverbial chasm or run into problems such as cash flow shortages, high employee turnover, or competitive price wars.

Steps 8 through 10 explain how to create the new infrastructure that is needed to take your company to cash flow positive and to an acquisition- or IPO-ready state and build the systems and processes needed to grow your organization, develop new products, and branch out into international markets. Part Three ends with a helpful review that provides 100 steps to building a company to $1 million in sales.

Part Three is an important section, especially for the younger entrepreneur. Covering the topic of personal development, it presents the strategies used by successful entrepreneurs. It covers the important skills of planning, goal setting, networking, having a bias toward action, and dealing with failure. The author explains his experience and what he has learned along his journey, and profiles the strategies for success used by many other successful entrepreneurs.

Zero to One Million is a book unlike any other on business or entrepreneurship. There have been books about entrepreneurship, books about economics, books about personal development, and case studies about successful companies, but never have these topics been combined in such a step-by-step, detailed guide.

Whether you are 16 with wide eyes and big dreams, 28 with an MBA and a vision, a 32-year-old mother of two, or 55 and venturing out on your own after a lifetime in the corporate world, this book will be an invaluable resource and inspiration.

Though nothing can ever be guaranteed without your action and perseverance, you will find steps within these pages that have been used time and time again to build companies to $1 million in sales and beyond. I wish you the best of luck as you begin your journey of building your own company toward its first million.

Sincerely yours,

Michael Simmons, Author
The Student Success Manifesto
Brooklyn, New York
November 2007

INTRODUCTION

I've seen a glimpse of the view from the fiftieth floor of the business skyscraper. There is a whole other world out there—a world of prosperity and unlimited wealth. I'd like to share what I have seen. I want you to be the person who creates further prosperity, jobs, and opportunity in your community. No matter where you're from, no matter who you are, no matter your access to opportunity or your background—you have the ability to become an extremely successful entrepreneur—with the right dedication, the right belief in yourself, and the right guide.

I wrote *Zero to One Million* in the hope of expanding access to entrepreneurial opportunity by sharing the steps to building a company from zero to over $1 million in sales. My hope is that this book can serve as a guide to helping you set your vision; take action; reach your biggest, hairiest, and most audacious goals; and turn your dreams and hard work into millions while creating jobs, developing a product or service used by thousands, and giving back to your community.

As part of this book, I am glad to be able to share with you the iContact story. iContact began in 2002 after my business partner, Aaron Houghton, and I met at a meeting of the Carolina Entrepreneurship Club. We set up shop in a two-room office in downtown Chapel Hill, North Carolina. We lived in the office, slept on a futon, cooked on a George Foreman Grill, ate lots of ramen noodles, and jumped in Dumpsters to get proof-of-purchase tags off of chair boxes for the $50 rebates at Staples.

We did whatever we had to to keep expenses low and get the company to the point where we had real revenue and people were willing to take us seriously. We bootstrapped for three years and then raised outside funding to accelerate growth. Today, Aaron and I are fortunate to have been able to bring on a rock-star team that has created a rapidly growing venture capital-backed company with over 80 employees and more than $10 million in annual sales.

I know of the desire in your mind to achieve, the passion in your heart, and the motivation in your soul. I can empathize with the struggles you are about to endure. I share what I know in the hope it can provide a guide on the path toward achieving business and financial success. If you are to succeed, you will experience drop-dead exhaustion and tireless passion caused by dedication to a dream, to people, to building something great. I understand it. I know it.

It can be extremely difficult to get started. Getting over the difficulty of people writing you off, turning you down, and telling you your dream will never come true is the first challenge of the entrepreneur. The keys I have found are to associate yourself with people who build you up and encourage your dreams, to write down your goals and frame them, and to take at least one positive action forward every day. A key message of this book is to get started today, regardless of your age, location, or position in life.

To share one of my favorite metaphors from Jim Collins's bestseller *Good to Great* (Collins, 2001), building a business is like pushing a big wooden wheel. The first push does next to nothing. Subsequent pushes barely move the wheel. Only continued effort in a single direction sustained over multiple months gets the wheel going at a decent clip. During this time of prolonged strain and few noticeable results, many people drop out of the game. You must have persistence in this game to win.

While very slow at first, eventually the big wheel starts to move. Soon the momentum of the energy and the inertia of the movement take over and the wheel begins to move by itself. The motion snowballs, and it begins spinning at a thousand revolutions per minute—faster and faster. Building a million-dollar company takes people, systems, commitment, and continued effort over multiple years.

It took us 35 months at iContact to build the company to $1 million in sales. I met my partner, Aaron Houghton, on October 2, 2002. On September 1, 2005, we made it to the $1 million in sales milestone. Time, focus, sacrifice, dedication, energy, and passion are required to play the game. To enter into the game, you must take action. The master painter Vincent van Gogh once said, "Great things are not done by impulse, but by a series of small things brought together."

To win at the game of entrepreneurship, we must always keep in mind that the true purpose of business is not to become a millionaire or make profits but rather to provide value to your customers, to create a positive impact, to innovate, to create great products, and to create jobs. Cash and profits should be seen as the lifeblood that allows you to strive after your company's true mission.

Today, we as humans have a tremendous opportunity to use our new communication tools, entrepreneurial talents, and money to work toward solving the biggest remaining issues in our world. I will spend the rest of my life working through entrepreneurship, social entrepreneurship, investing, philanthropy, public policy, and politics to end poverty and hunger in developing nations and at home, ensure environmental sustainability, help world leaders understand that we are one humanity and that our commonalities are much greater than our differences, and expand access to opportunity, health care, and education in every nation. This book is a first step in this mission that I hope to work toward over the next six decades.

I thank you for picking up a copy of *Zero to One Million* and hope you have the opportunity to use it as your guide as you work toward building an extremely successful venture. I hope I have conveyed an interesting story while providing a guide that will enable you to reach your dreams. If I succeed in this goal, all I ask is that you spread the word, give back, and take a positive action every day toward your greater vision.

My sincere regards,

Ryan P.M. Allis
November 2007
Chapel Hill, North Carolina

P.S.—Please do stay in touch. I can be reached via ryan@icontact.com or via Facebook. I am happy to help in any way that I can.

Part One

★

MY STORY: GOING FROM ZERO TO ONE MILLION

1

GETTING OFF THE GROUND

Until one is committed, there is hesitancy, the chance to draw back. . . . A whole stream of events issues from the decision, raising in one's favor all manner of unforeseen incidents and meetings and material assistance, which no man could have dreamed would have come his way. Whatever you can do, or dream you can do, begin it. Boldness has genius, power, and magic in it. Begin it now.

—W. H. MURRAY, SCOTTISH MOUNTAINEER

Who I Am

I am the son of an Episcopalian priest from Pennsylvania and a social worker from England. I was born in Pennsylvania in 1984 and grew up in Pennsylvania, Rhode Island, and Florida. When I was 11, I received a Macintosh LC computer from my Uncle Steve, who lived in Massachusetts at the time. I learned everything I could about that computer. I even traded in my airline frequent-flyer miles to subscribe to the computer magazine *PC World*, which I would read in its entirety. I used the computer daily and loved to play great games like SimCity and Cannon Fodder.

The next summer I was thinking about what I could do to earn extra money while school was out. My family and I were then living on Anna Maria Island, just off the coast of Bradenton, Florida. I realized that I had become pretty good at setting up and troubleshooting computers and that there were a number of senior citizens in our area who were starting to purchase them to access e-mail and the Internet.

So I placed a free classified ad in the island newspaper: "Need Computer Help? Call Ryan at 555–6406 for Onsite Help from Responsible 12 year old. Just $5/hour." I also placed flyers at the local post office, city hall, the library, the laundromat, and the Chamber of Commerce. I even put flyers in mailboxes, but I had to stop because the postmaster general wasn't too happy.

After a couple days of anxiously waiting, my phone began to ring. I scheduled my first appointment that Saturday with Fred from 45th Street. I did one hour of work with Fred, and he paid me $10. The first week on the job when I got a call from Fred's friend Betty from 67th Street, I learned my first important business lesson: word-of-mouth marketing is the best type of marketing you can have.

That summer my business did pretty well, and I began to understand the power of word of mouth. There weren't too many 12-year-olds offering computer help at the time, and my services became a topic of conversation at retirement homes, country clubs, and church services. I printed up business cards and made sure to give at least five to every client. By the end of the summer I had earned $463, an amazing amount in my young eyes.

> "The first week on the job I learned my first important business lesson: word-of-mouth marketing is the best type of marketing you can have."

The following summer, now a teenager, I once again placed my ads and contacted my client base. I began installing memory, giving purchasing advice, and teaching clients how to use e-mail and the Internet. Now, however, I could charge $8 per hour because of the higher demand for my services, the spreading word of mouth, and my additional experience. By the end of the summer I felt enormously wealthy, having earned $1,200. I socked away most of these earnings in a mutual fund.

In November 1997, my eighth-grade year, my family moved from Anna Maria Island to the mainland about five miles to the east. Fortunately, I was still able to go to the same school and remained close enough to my client base. In the second semester, I learned HTML, the basic computer language used to create Web sites. This knowledge would prove very useful down the road.

My First Clients

The next June, I once again distributed my flyers, and invested $12 each week for a classified ad in the mainland paper. It was now 1998, and I had gained considerable knowledge about computers. Halfway through the summer, a lady by the name of Lois gave me a call. She had a problem with her laptop and needed it fixed. After I had fixed the problem, she told me that she was interested in setting up a Web page and wanted to know if I could do it. I told her that I had not had much experience, but I'd give it a shot and see what I could remember from my HTML class.

It turned out that Lois was a flight attendant, and she brought back pearl rings, pendants, and necklaces every month when she flew to China. After a few months of successfully selling the pearls to her friends, she decided she wanted to try selling them through the Internet. To get going, we registered a domain name for her pearl business, obtained a merchant account, and purchased an online shopping cart. She had photographs taken of her products and wrote descriptions for each.

Her sales started slowly, as I was not too far along the learning curve. Within a month, however, Freshwaterpearls.com had a full e-business running, with 70 products available online. I optimized the pages for the search engines, started a monthly sweepstakes, and posted articles about pearls to the site. We began a monthly newsletter, *The Pearl Ezine,* and within six months it had 5,300 subscribers. We started making three or four sales a day, and my design and marketing skills continued to improve.

However, we soon ran into trouble. It was difficult for Lois to keep track of inventory, send out orders on time, and take care of customer service while continuing as a flight attendant, which took her out of the country for two weeks at a time. Customer communication, the supply chain, and customer service were not at the level they needed to be.

The company reached a critical point: would Lois hire her first employee and attempt to build a true business with systems and processes, or would she continue to try to run everything herself? This problem is, of course, the classic dilemma of the small business entrepreneur. She decided to try to continue to run everything herself.

Unfortunately, after nine months or so, both the site and the business folded. At the same time, I had learned much more about business, e-commerce, and Web design than I ever would have in a classroom, and this experience would later prove to be a great asset.

From this experience, I learned my second important business lesson: when your business is making enough revenue to be able to hire an employee, make the leap and bring on your first team member. Otherwise, you will be building a job for yourself rather than a true business.

> "When your business is making enough revenue to be able to hire an employee, make the leap and bring on your first team member. Otherwise, you will be building a job for yourself rather than a true business."

During my freshman and sophomore years in high school, I continued learning about Web design and development. After developing a couple sites of my own, I took over developing the Web site for my high school during my sophomore year.

The summer after tenth grade I was lucky enough to be selected as one of six U.S. ambassadors to La Ruta Quetzal, which entailed a 53-day expedition to Spain and Mexico conducted entirely in Spanish and sponsored by the government of Spain and brought together 350 students from 43 countries. I would have to put off my entrepreneurial endeavors for a couple months.

The Birth of Virante

On June 20, 2000, I left for Madrid. I had traveled in Western Europe previously but had not been to Spain. Upon arriving in Spain I met up with the other students and staff. We slept outside in tents each night, and each day we would either hike or take a bus to a different town. Eighteen-hour days and weekly 30-mile hikes were the norm. By the time we finished in Mexico City on August 11, 2000, I had made some great friends and enjoyed some amazing experiences.

I mention this trip because a very important thing occurred while I was in a park in Mexico City on the last night of the trip. I had my first entrepreneurial brainstorming session. I was about to return home and figured it was time to develop a business plan for the next year. During this session I came up with the name Virante (pronounced: Vih-rahn-tay). I honestly do not remember how or why, but somehow it ended up on my paper. I said to myself, "I like that. I guess it does sound a bit Spanish." And so it stuck. I planned to start a Web design and development firm by the name of Virante when I arrived back in Florida.

A few days later I returned to school. The first day of eleventh grade was my sixteenth birthday, and I could finally drive! No longer would I have to beg to be driven around or ride my bike to appointments. Each day after coming home from cross-country practice and on the weekends I would work on Virante. I registered my Web site and began designing the site, adding my portfolio and resume, creating a Flash intro, and promoting my new company, Virante Design & Development.

I didn't know a thing about S corporations, limited liability companies (LLCs), 83(b) elections, equity, stock options, or tax laws. That knowledge would come later. However, I was skilled at graphic design, Web site development, and e-commerce integration. During my junior year I used and improved these skills as I picked up a few new clients. I built Web sites for a land development company, an on-site medical care company, a film company, a dating service, a travel agency, and a painting company. I also designed business cards, brochures, and logos, and consulted on marketing Web sites.

I knew little about contracts, marketing offline, or billing processes. Once I almost had a multi-thousand-dollar contract to revamp the AutoZone Web site but lost out simply because I showed my inexperience by asking what they meant by "2/10 net 30," which I soon thereafter learned is the term for a discounted and full payment on an invoice. However, I was learning. Some of my clients needed database work done that was a bit too advanced for me at the time, so I formed a partnership with a programming firm in Nevada. I outsourced this work to them and they sent some of their design work to me. This partnership ended up working out very well and taught me the value of strategic alliances.

I began bidding on projects through sites such as guru.com and smarterwork.com, and I picked up one client in Miami and another in Leicester, England. By the middle of the summer of 2001 I had created about 10 Web sites and had worked with about 20 companies in one way or another. Everything was going quite well, and once again word of mouth was spreading.

I read in a marketing book about the benefit of sending out press releases, so in about the middle of July that year I decided to write a press release on what I was doing and send it to the local papers. This turned out to be one of the most fortunate decisions I ever made. On July 26, 2001, I was featured on the front page of the *Bradenton Herald*. I had absolutely no idea I'd be on the front page, and I was taken aback when I saw my picture right on top in the newspaper rack while walking into Wal-Mart that morning.

I had 17 messages on my machine by noon on July 26, every one of them wanting me to develop their Web site.

This overload presented a problem. I could not possibly create 17 Web sites at once; the most I had ever previously worked on at the same time was three. I called each prospect back and scheduled appointments with the most promising clients. On August 1, I thought that I would be set for new work for the next few months. By August 3, this reality had changed.

Landing the Job

At the same time the front-page article appeared, the owner of a local company in Holmes Beach, Florida, saw my small, 20-word ad offering computer help in the island newspaper and gave me a call. I set up an appointment with him the next day. When I walked into his office, I noticed materials for Corey Rudl's marketing course on the counter. I commented to the owner, "Oh yeah, I read through that course a couple years ago. Good stuff." I went on to fix a broken disk drive in his computer, and we talked a bit about his business.

It turned out that he had just let his Web designer go, and he needed a new one. I ran to my car to get a copy of the newspaper article from a few days earlier, and he said, "So when do you want to start?"

The business owner had been developing a product for a couple years and was just beginning to promote it. He wanted me to set up a Web site for the product and a system for customers to order the product online. I told him I could do it.

On August 14, 2001, the first day of my senior year of high school and my seventeenth birthday, I began work. I had been able to convince my school to give me an internship class for the last two periods each day, so I was able to work from noon until about 7 p.m. at the company's office. After I finished the Web site, I was to begin promoting the Web site and encouraging sales of the product. I would work as an independent contractor for tax purposes, though unofficially my title would be vice president of marketing.

When we began, the company had not made a single sale through their Web site. They were selling only a few hundred dollars' worth of product each month to a handful of retail customers and one health food store to which they sold the product at wholesale. It would take another two weeks before we made our first sale through the Web site. Sales came slowly at first. The company did $1,500 in September 2001 and $5,600 in October 2001.

By April 2002, the company was doing over $85,000 in sales each month, and in the fall of 2002, the company passed $1 million in total sales. The company was fortunate to be able to reach this milestone without any venture capital funding or debt, bank loans, or private investment, and with just one product and five employees.

At the age of 17, I had the opportunity to see a company grow from nothing to over $1 million in sales in just over a year. I learned a lot from managing a monthly marketing budget of about $50,000 and seeing the company grow from two to six employees. This ex-

> "What I was learning about financing, payroll, bank relations, product positioning, and human resources would help me tremendously when I did set out to be an entrepreneur myself."

perience was essentially my internship. I did not yet realize I was an entrepreneur—I viewed myself as a marketer, but what I was learning about financing, payroll, bank relations, product positioning, and human resources would help me tremendously when I did set out to be an entrepreneur myself.

At the end of the year, I made the decision to go to Chapel Hill, North Carolina, to begin my first year of college at the University of North Carolina (UNC).

2

BECOMING AN ENTREPRENEUR

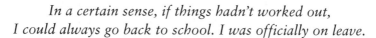

In a certain sense, if things hadn't worked out,
I could always go back to school. I was officially on leave.

—BILL GATES 1974

The Decision to Go to College

At 5:00 a.m. on August 14, 2002, my eighteenth birthday, I got into a rented white PT Cruiser with my dad and drove up to Chapel Hill, North Carolina. I was to begin college at the University of North Carolina in five days. Although the decision to go to college was difficult to make, especially after the success we had had with the health products company in high school, I felt it was the best choice for me, based on my long-term goals.

Just a few months earlier, in April 2002, I was sitting on the floor of my living room in Bradenton, Florida, with four acceptance letters laid out in front of me. After visiting each college and receiving the financial aid information, I decided on UNC—Chapel Hill because the cost was considerably lower than that of New York University and it was outside the state, unlike the University of Florida. However, the success at the health products company presented me with a new decision to make. Should I even go to college at all?

I was a good student and had a chance to receive a near-full ride to a great university, so why would I even consider not going? Well, it was April and I saw that the company I was working for was taking off. I knew that if I deferred college for a year, I had the chance to make quite a bit of money. I had to make a choice. Should I accept admission from UNC or defer? I had until August to make my final decision.

During that summer, I met two young people who had deferred admission to their respective colleges and had built very successful companies. I knew I could do the same. I feared that college would prepare me to work for someone else, and I knew that I did not want to work for anyone but myself. I felt that in college, my time would be taken up learning things I would never use and I would be in a constant battle to maintain a high grade point average in order to get a good job someday, which didn't appeal to me. I thought I had the skills and resources to succeed without college. I would develop some software and informational products, and my career as an in-demand author, consultant, successful entrepreneur, and investor would be launched. I knew I could do it.

However, I wanted something more than this. I believed there was much more to life than money. Further, I was not sure that I could survive the psychological stress of being 18 and not having a single friend younger than 27. I considered that going to college, at least for a year or two, would probably help me develop my network and learn to live on my own. So I chose to go off to UNC.

Although I often became frustrated at not having enough time to work on my businesses or read what I wanted to read, I know the choice I made was what was best for me. College made me go through many formative and developmental changes.

Just as important, I developed a network of contacts and built strong relationships that have been a great asset to me. I found other students like myself, made some friends, and found a partner among these friends with whom I would later start iContact.

The Carolina Entrepreneurship Club

During my first semester in college I discovered the Carolina Entrepreneurship Club (CEC). At the Master Panel of Entrepreneurs event hosted by UNC in mid-September I met a man by the name of Jeff Reid, who was the executive director of the Center for Entrepreneurship at UNC. He suggested I talk to Paul Vollman, an undergraduate who, along with a few others, was in the process of starting an undergraduate entrepreneurship club. Jeff thought that I should get involved.

I e-mailed Paul, telling him I wanted to help, and we set up a meeting right away. He appointed me the tech chair for the club, which meant I was responsible for the Web site and listserv. The first meeting would be in two weeks.

The smell of chicken nuggets and honey mustard permeated the room as I walked into the first CEC meeting on October 5, 2002. About 25 students showed up to hear two local men, entrepreneur Todd Ballenger and private equity businessman Hunter Bost, talk about their experiences and the differences between entrepreneurship and intrapreneurship. At that first meeting I was introduced to someone who would play a key role in my life. His name was Aaron Houghton, a senior computer science major at UNC.

When I met Aaron that night, he already knew who I was, as I had created a Web discussion forum for UNC that was featured in the school newspaper. Being a Web developer, he kept close tabs on the other Web designers and developers at the school. Aaron's company, Preation, Inc., had been around since 1998. As his business expanded in his sophomore year, he moved his offices to a 700-square-foot, four-room location right in the heart of downtown Chapel Hill, at the intersection of Franklin Street and Columbia Street. We met, and he invited me to his office the next weekend.

At his office that weekend, Aaron showed me a few of the software products he had developed for his clients, one of which, the Preation Email List Manager, caught my eye. The company I had worked with in my senior year in high school used a desktop-based program called Mailloop to send out their e-mail newsletter. While Mailloop worked well initially, it eventually proved to be too slow. Even using the company's broadband connection, it would often take 24 hours or more for the newsletter to be sent, completely tying up all the resources of a company computer during this time.

The software Aaron had developed, however, was Web based, meaning that it could be accessed from any computer with an Internet connection anywhere in the world; once you composed your message and hit Send, you would be done right away. You could close your browser and go on to other work while the server sent out the e-mails within a matter of minutes. In addition, Aaron's software had some other features that made it unique in comparison to the alternatives on the market at that time. Furthermore, at the entry level it cost only $10 per month rather than the $400 up-front cost of Mailloop. It was simply a better solution, and, since my entrepreneurial mind is always running, I saw the possibilities immediately.

At that meeting, I agreed to work with Aaron to develop the software from a beta version used by a handful of his customers to a commercial version that would attract and handle thousands of customers. Leveraging this software for which there was a demonstrated need in the marketplace, my experience in Web marketing and business development, and Aaron's programming abilities, we would have a good opportunity to build a profitable product line for Preation.

Virante, Inc.

Since August 2000, when I returned from Mexico City, I had been operating under the name of Virante Design & Development as a sole proprietorship. Now it was time to formalize things. I was about to enter into a contract to market software that had a chance to bring in a significant amount of revenue, and I wanted to reduce my liability exposure as well as lay the foundation for the company to grow. During the fall semester break, I incorporated Virante, Inc., as a North Carolina corporation and filled out Form 2553 from the Internal Revenue Service to elect to be an S corporation, which provides certain tax advantages for small businesses.

Three weeks later, I received the Articles of Incorporation for Virante from Elaine Marshall, secretary of state for North Carolina. I was finally the chief executive officer of a real incorporated company. My official company headquarters was 610 Ehringhaus Dorm, although I often worked at Aaron's offices.

I formed Virante, Inc., not to do Web site design, as I had done before, but rather to do Web marketing consulting and search engine optimization, as well as to engage in a joint venture with Preation to sell the e-mail list management software.

On the weekends I began to work with Aaron to build and improve the software. We first had to come up with a better name for the product. We sat down for a couple hours and brainstormed. We wrote down words related to the functions of the software and then generated every possibility we could think of. Eventually, we came up with the name IntelliContact (in June 2007, the name was shortened to iContact, which I will use to refer to the product from here on). We checked to make sure the domain name was available and then checked with the U.S. Patent and Trademark Office to make sure the name had not already been trademarked.

Once these two things were cleared, we decided to go with the name. We registered the Web site and transferred the Web-based software to the new site. We had a logo designed, designed the site, and added sales copy, feature descriptions, related white papers, and FAQs to the site. We also created a Flash tour, obtained a security certificate, started the process of obtaining a merchant account so we could accept credit cards, and began work on the back-end programming of the shopping cart and affiliate program. Aaron and I also worked out a contract whereby Virante would work to market the iContact software in exchange for a percentage of the sales.

MBA Classes at 18

Over the next five months a few things happened that changed our direction in selling the iContact software. I was initially told by the head of the undergraduate business program that there was no way he would allow a freshman to do an independent study, but I eventually was able to convince him, after explaining my prior experience and the knowledge I had gained from that. Because I had established a good relationship with Jeff Reid from the Center for Entrepreneurship at UNC, he agreed to be my faculty advisor for an independent study in entrepreneurship during the second semester.

The curriculum for the independent study consisted of writing a case study, reading two textbooks on entrepreneurship, interviewing six experienced entrepreneurs, and sitting in on three MBA classes at Kenan-Flagler Business School. It was this last requirement that most excited me.

The first half of the semester—or "first mod," as it is called—I sat in on BUSI 299Q, Venture Capital Deal Structure and Valuation, and BUSI 221L, Legal Issues for High Technology Start-ups. For the second mod, I sat in on BUSI 296S, Managing a Small Business. Except for some of the math in the venture capital valuation class, these classes were a good match for my knowledge level. Legal Issues for High Technology Start-ups was an especially helpful class. It was taught by Merrill Mason, an adjunct professor and practicing attorney with Hutchison & Mason, PLLC, which later became the law firm for iContact.

As part of the independent study, I also started the Distinguished Entrepreneur Interview Series. To be interviewed, an entrepreneur had to be the CEO or founder of a company that was doing more than $5 million in annual sales. I teamed up with Jeff Reid and leveraged the network of the Center for Entrepreneurship to identify participants. I found that there was no better way to build my own network, as well as increase my knowledge about what I needed to do to get to the next level, than talking with these entrepreneurs.

To complete the course requirements, I also studied in detail the texts, *New Venture Creation,* by Jeffrey Timmons, which I highly recommend, and *Entrepreneurship,* by Donald F. Kuratko and Richard M. Hodgetts.

In addition to the independent study and MBA classes, I had been elected vice president of the Carolina Entrepreneurship Club for a second semester. We had a speaker series event each month, signed the Club Constitution on February 24, 2003, and began to host other types of events such as Business Roundtables, Legal Help-Desks, and Start-up Clinics. By the end of the second semester we had 53 dues-paying members and were hosting two events per month. In late April, I was elected president of the club and began working on plans and goals for the upcoming school year.

I had come to Chapel Hill in August 2002 as someone who knew Web marketing and a bit about business development. At the health products company in high school I had handled the Web site, the affiliate program, the marketing campaign, and the customer relations. I had also gained experience in cash flow management, human resources, income statements, balance sheets, budgeting, and product development. The owner had developed the product, managed the financing, and dealt with the bank, payroll, bookkeeping, inventory, and supply chain management. While I had acquired more experience than anyone would expect of a 17-year-old, I still felt, coming in to UNC, that I was mainly a marketer and not an entrepreneur. I wanted to become a full-fledged entrepreneur.

By taking accounting first semester, incorporating Virante, being the vice president of the Carolina Entrepreneurship Club and attending the speaker series meetings, building my business resource site at www.zeromillion.com, reading two entrepreneurship textbooks, interviewing successful entrepreneurs, and sitting in on those three MBA classes, I had made good progress toward becoming a true entrepreneur. While my core competency remained in Web marketing, I now had experience in company formation and knowledge about raising capital, developing products, managing employees, and bookkeeping.

Unlike that day in 2001 when I lost the AutoZone contract, I now had the fundamental business knowledge I needed to become a full-fledged entrepreneur. In the intervening years, I had learned

> "I now had the fundamental business knowledge I needed to become a full-fledged entrepreneur. However, I had to test my ability as an entrepreneur in the real world."

about equity, noncompete contracts, nondisclosure agreements, cash flow, income statements, balance sheets, nonqualified stock options, 83(b) elections, C and S corporations, venture capital (VC) traunches, FICA, angel investors, pro formas, down-rounds, term sheets, and internal rates of return. However, I had to test my ability as an entrepreneur in the real world. It was time to build a company of my own to $1 million in sales rather than doing it for someone else. And so the journey began.

Starting iContact

Based on what we learned in the Legal Issues for High Technology Start-ups class, Aaron and I decided to change the way we would structure the business foundation for the iContact software. Instead of selling the software as a product of Preation, we decided, in March 2003, to incorporate a new company that would sell it. We chose to do this for three reasons.

First, the new entity would make it much easier for us to sort out ownership in the company. It would have been confusing to distribute equity in the company when Preation's main business was Web site development, not e-mail marketing software. Second, the accounting of expenses and payroll would have been more complex if we hadn't restructured the business. Without a clear idea of our revenue and expenses and how much we needed to make to break even, planning and spending for iContact would have been more difficult.

Finally, we wanted the advantage of having a company that could one day be sold or acquired without affecting the business operations of Preation. We knew that the best ways to accomplish our goals of building a great product, creating a lot of jobs, and building shareholder value were to form a separate company, build a great team, attract a few thousand customers, expand our product line, and then sell to another company or go public. We would be able to do this only if everything was clear and properly separated from the start.

We started this process with a visit to our lawyer on April 15, 2003. Merrill Mason, who taught the Legal Issues class, was a well-known lawyer for entrepreneurial ventures in the area, so we decided to talk to him. Merrill gave a free initial consultation, during which he outlined the process for forming the company. Aaron and I had already incorporated a company before, but incorporating a company with more than one shareholder (we had five, initially) is much more complex. Although the approach we took ended up costing us $3,000 instead of the $300 it would have cost to do it online, doing it properly turned out to be worth every penny.

Merrill told us that before our next meeting, we would have to come up with a company name and decide the breakdown of ownership. He also told us about the noncompete, nondisclosure, confidentiality, consulting, employment, and stock restriction agreements we would have to sign in addition to the company bylaws, stock options plan, organizational consent, 83(b) elections, and Certificate of Authority that were necessary.

For a look into a typical day in the life of a young entrepreneur, check out www.zeromillion.com/young/entrepreneurial-day.html.

Aaron and I came back from the lawyer's office and got to work deciding on the equity share and thinking of a name for the company. Often, one of the most difficult early-stage decisions for an entrepreneur is what to name the company. The fact that five people (our initial shareholders) had to agree on the name complicated the process exponentially.

We began by brainstorming and compiling a list of all the potential names we could think of. We came up with names such as Alatro, Aspensmith, Calprion, Chapelsoft, Dyneap, Mobilardi, Preasio, Reactera, Redsync, and Sentelis. We wanted a name that sounded like it belonged to a technology company, but was not so high-tech that it would seem destined to fail like so many dot-coms and IT companies did between 2000 and 2002. We took our initial list of 300 possibilities and cross-referenced it first against domain name registrations and then against the U.S. Patent and Trademark Office's trademark database. Once this was done, we ended up with about 50 possibilities. Everyone in the office voted, and then we discussed the names as a group.

At first we could not find a name that we all agreed on, so we went through the process a second time. We brainstormed another 300 names and, after checking them, ended up with 50 more possibilities. We voted once more, and then finally decided on a name from the first round: Broadwick. Calprion was the second-place name, and Sentelis came in third. In all, we spent about 12 hours over four weeks coming up with the name. We changed the name of the company from Broadwick Corp. to iContact Corp. in July 2007 to align our product name with our company name.

By May 2003, Aaron and I had finished school, and my journey as a full-time entrepreneur had begun.

An Entrepreneurial Summer

Although we now had the name finalized, we had yet to settle on the equity distribution among myself as CEO, Aaron as chief technology officer and chairman, Erik as systems administrator, Charles, as vice president of marketing, Wes was network administrator, and Preation, which would transfer ownership of the software to iContact.

The three main parties involved were Aaron, Charles, and myself, as Wes and Erik would only be working part-time for the company.

for insight into the initial work in starting a company, check out www.zeromillion.com/young/life-as-an-entrepreneur.html to read my essay "My First Week as an Entrepreneur."

Aaron and I negotiated between ourselves, and then I negotiated with Charles. After we settled on percentages, salaries, accrual formulas, and bonuses, we offered equity to Erik and Wes. Once they were in agreement, we returned to Hutchison & Mason, PLLC, on July 1 to formally incorporate iContact as a Delaware C corporation. Corporate documents are processed much faster in Delaware than in North Carolina, so by the next day, we had a company. The formation process was far from complete, however.

A few weeks later, on August 4, 2003, we returned to Hutchison & Mason to review the formation documents. There were 33 documents in all, including five noncompete, nondisclosure, and confidentiality agreements; three consulting agreements; two employment agreements; four stock restriction agreements; one promissory note; a board consent for the promissory note; a stock options agreement; the company bylaws; an organizational consent; four 83(b) elections; a nonqualified stock option agreement; an application for a certificate of authority; an assignment of inventions; a stock ledger; a capitalization chart; an organizational checklist; and four stock certificates. It is a much more complex process when forming a company with more than one shareholder.

By mid-August, we finally had the documents signed. We were an official company. We already had quite a bit of momentum, however; since October 2002, and throughout the process of forming the company, we were working full-time on improving the software, building the Web sites, writing sales copy, presenting at trade shows, obtaining a merchant account, and launching our affiliate and search engine optimization campaigns. By the time the documents were signed, we had 20 paying customers and 100 affiliates who promoted our software in exchange for a commission on every sale they referred.

During the summer I also attended two 10-day Lead America Business & Entrepreneurship Conferences to teach entrepreneurship to high school students. I had the time of my life, first in Washington, D.C., for training and then in Chicago and Boston for the conferences. I wrote about this in an article available online at http://www.zeromillion.com/young/teaching-entrepreneurship.html.

The summer of 2003 was one that I will never forget. I had a great time, living at my office and sleeping on the futon, launching iContact, and traveling to Chicago and Boston to teach entrepreneurship to high schoolers. I lived the life of the bootstrapping entrepreneur, and I loved it.

At the end of the summer, I moved into an apartment two miles from the office. Chapel Hill was again abuzz with 25,000 students, and the Carolina Entrepreneurship Club was back in session. It was time to build iContact.

From Zero to One Million

The marketing campaign had launched in early July, and by the end of the summer, we had 20 paying customers for iContact. Charles and I were working full-time on increasing the number of affiliates we had and building links to our informational Web site, while Aaron worked on adding new features to the software.

Unfortunately for the company, Charles left in August to pursue a new venture. We were in need of someone to take over his marketing role so we could continue the affiliate and search engine optimization campaign. Fortunately for us, our offices were across the street from UNC—Chapel Hill. We put up flyers in the business school and within three days received two resumes. We ended up offering an internship to Josh Carlton, a 2003 University of Richmond graduate who happened to see our flyer while at the business school with his girlfriend, who was starting on her master's degree in accounting.

At this point we had been working for a full year, determining our business strategy, forming the company, developing the software, and implementing our sales model. Now, it came down to execution and whether I could evolve from simply a marketing consultant into an experienced entrepreneur and manager.

By October 2003, iContact had over 50 paying customers. Josh had done well and became our director of marketing. Our Web site was among the top listings of the major search engines for "e-mail marketing" and "e-mail marketing software," and we had recruited over 200 affiliates who promoted our product online in exchange for a percentage of the sales revenue.

In November 2003, David Roth joined the team as vice president of business development after seeing an article about iContact in the local newspaper. At age 57, David was the first "gray-hair" to sign on, and he helped us gain credibility. By the end of 2003, we had booked a grand total of $11,964 in sales and had 78 paying customers. We had gone from nonexistent to an operating and growing entity with four full-time employees. Though the initial growth took longer than we had anticipated, we were on our way. We ended 2004 with $296,000 in sales, 12 employees, and 1,200 paying customers.

My goal since age 18 had been to build a company to $1 million in sales before my twenty-first birthday. After 35 months of building iContact, we hit that milestone on September 1, 2005. I missed my deadline by 18 days, but I was still elated. iContact was now a million-dollar company.

> "By the end of 2003, we had booked a grand total of $11,964 in sales and had 78 paying customers. We had gone from nonexistent to an operating and growing entity with four full-time employees. Though the initial growth took longer than we had anticipated, we were on our way."

Venture Funding

We ended 2005 with $1.3 million in sales, 22 employees, and 3,600 paying customers. We ended 2006 with $2.9 million in sales, 37 employees, and 7,600 paying customers. We ended 2007 with $6.8 million in sales, 75 employees, and 18,000 paying customers.

When we began in 2003, our goal at iContact was to build the company to $1 million in sales. When we reached that mark in September 2005, we had to make the choice whether to sell the company or raise outside capital to grow further. We chose to begin the process of raising funding.

In May 2006, after three years of bootstrapping the company, we chose to raise a seed round of $500,000 in funding from a local venture capital firm in Durham called NC IDEA. After turning down a term sheet from another local firm due to disagreeing on terms, we ended up raising the funds from NC IDEA as convertible debt, which converted into equity ownership in May 2007 at an agreed-upon multiple of trailing twelve-month (TTM) revenues. Part Two of this book discusses both the fund-raising process and how to scale customer acquisition and create the marketing, human resource, and technical systems needed to make growth possible.

After this first round of financing, sales grew rapidly. Sales increased from $180,000 per month prior to the investment in May 2006 to over $530,000 per month in May 2007. To enable the growth, we launched a fully redesigned version of iContact in August 2006 that included the ability to create e-mail newsletters, surveys, autoresponders, blogs, and RSS feeds. We also invested heavily in online advertising.

As our software became more robust, we began selling up-market and added Fortune 500 companies like AT&T, Bank of America, and International Paper to our client list. We began adding more experienced members to our team, including Chief Financial Officer Tim Oakley, Director of Communications Chuck Hester, Director of Human Resources Cindy Hays, and Director of Sales Matt Allen. We also began getting significant trade and press coverage with the launch of our new version in August 2006 and were featured in *Fortune Small Business, Success Magazine,* and *Entrepreneur* and on CNBC's *The Big Idea with Donny Deutsch.*

In the spring of 2007, we had to make the "scale or sell" choice once again. We could sell the company to a strategic acquirer or raise additional capital in order to fund bringing on a world-class management team and further funding customer acquisition. We decided to raise additional funds so that we could grow faster and have a chance at either an eventual public offering or a large strategic acquisition. We went out on the road again and pitched 39 venture firms starting in January 2007. We received offers from four venture firms to invest in our second round, which we referred to as our Series A round, since our first round was small.

In June 2007, iContact raised $5.25 million from a firm in Reston, Virginia, called Updata Partners and our original partner, NC IDEA, and $100,000 from a local investor. Since then, our growth has continued at a rapid pace, and we now have over a $10 million annual run rate. We've continued to add great people to the team and are building toward what we hope will be an eventual large strategic acquisition or public offering. Our annual sales since company inception are shown in Figure 2.1.

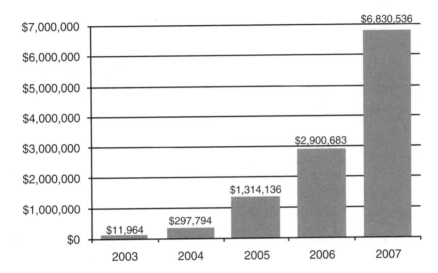

Figure 2.1 iContact annual sales since company inception.

My story ends here for now. I hope it has provided insight that will be helpful in launching and growing your own company and reaching your goals. But first, you'll need a guide to get there. Part Two explains the knowledge needed to become a successful entrepreneur and provides a 10-step process for building your own company to over $1 million in sales.

Part Two

★

THE 10-STEP PROCESS FOR BUILDING A COMPANY TO $1 MILLION IN SALES

3

STEP 1:

UNDERSTAND THE SYSTEM

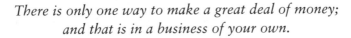

*There is only one way to make a great deal of money;
and that is in a business of your own.*

—J. PAUL GETTY, ONCE THE RICHEST MAN IN AMERICA

The Role of the Entrepreneur in the Market System

Let's start things off with a question. What is needed to create wealth? Within the marketplace, there are many resources that go into the production of goods and services. These resources can be grouped into four categories: *land, labor, capital,* and *entrepreneurial ability.*

The resource of entrepreneurial ability is where you come into play. It is the entrepreneur who organizes and arranges the use of land, labor, and capital to create an output demanded by the marketplace. It is the entrepreneur's responsibility to decide on what amounts of each resource to use and then use those resources efficiently to create a product or service that is valued more highly by the marketplace than the collective value of the resource inputs. As Campbell R. McConnell and Stanley L. Brue say in *Economics,* "Both a sparkplug and a catalyst, the entrepreneur is at once the driving force behind production and the agent who combines the other resources in what is hoped will be a profitable venture."

The entrepreneur is the catalyst that brings together the resources of land, labor, and capital to create valuable goods and services in the hopes of building a profitable business. The word *entrepreneur* is of French origin and derives from *entreprendre,* which means "to undertake." The *American Heritage Dictionary* defines an entrepreneur as "a person who organizes, operates, and assumes the risk for a business venture."

The entrepreneur plays a vital role in society. Without entrepreneurs, there would be no businesses, no inventions, no innovation, no progress, and no wealth. Without the entrepreneur and the system that provides incentives for entrepreneurs, we would have no printing press, no bifocals, no airplane, no air conditioner, no radio, no microwave, no computer, no telephone, no television, and no George Foreman Lean Mean Fat-Burning Grilling Machine. Our standard of living would not be much better than that of 1450. The world would not be able to support the 6.5 billion people that it does, and the Malthusian doomsday predictions of overpopulation would have been realized many decades, if not centuries, ago.

> "Without the entrepreneur and the system that provides incentives for entrepreneurs, we would have no printing press, no bifocals, no airplane, no air conditioner, no radio, no microwave, no computer, no telephone, no television, and no George Foreman Lean Mean Fat-Burning Grilling Machine."

If it is your goal to become an entrepreneur, whether by running a small business in your hometown or by launching a high-potential venture with VC funding, you should be commended. While being an entrepreneur is surely not for everybody, if you are the type of person who has a bias toward action, who brings efficiency and innovation into everything you do, who creates systems and processes, is not afraid to make mistakes, can build and inspire a quality team, and will persist until pigs fly in a frozen-over hell while the cows come home and the Cubs win the pennant, you have what it takes to be a successful entrepreneur.

How the System of Entrepreneurship Works

There is an entirely different world out there—a world of prosperity and unlimited wealth. You can enter this world, if you are aware it exists. To enter this world, you must understand how the system of entrepreneurship works.

There are two ways to build wealth through entrepreneurship. The first way is to build a business and pay yourself a salary. If your business grows large enough to have an ample net profit margin, you can reinvest part in your company and still have enough to pay yourself a large salary and take out any profits as dividends each year.

You may personally earn a few hundred thousand dollars per year, and you might be happy with this amount, at all times maintaining majority ownership in your company and doing things the way you like to do them while still making time for other commitments such as family. This method of becoming wealthy is often associated with that of the lifestyle entrepreneur, small business owner, family business owner, and the S corporation. It is surely one option, and over time, these types of companies can grow to become large organizations.

The second way to build wealth through entrepreneurship is to build a high-potential company and make the majority of your money when the company goes public or sells to another company. By building, scaling, and then selling or taking public a high-potential company, the successful entrepreneur can end up earning tens of millions of dollars for changing an industry and bringing immense value to a customer base. To accomplish this goal, you'll have to develop a novel product or technology or partner with someone who has, protect your intellectual property, and build a great team. You'll need to write a business plan and get the right introductions so you can get in front of accredited private investors, angel investors, or venture capitalists. You'll also need to be willing to give up a portion of ownership to the investors.

You'll have to bring on a top-tier team, in turn giving up a good part of the remaining ownership to your founders and top performers. You'll need to bring on additional products, build systems and processes, outsource operations across the globe, launch international marketing campaigns, use derivatives to hedge risk in overseas currency markets, and attract seasoned executives and MBAs to your growing firm.

You'll need to attract a solid board of directors led by representatives of your investors and industry leaders. And you'll have to reach proof of concept, raise a second and third round of financing, ensure that your books meet the standards of generally accepted accounting principles (GAAP), create a product management system, scale customer acquisition, expand market share, build a sales system, and turn profitable.

> "You'll need to attract a solid board of directors led by representatives of your investors and industry leaders. And you'll have to reach proof of concept, raise a second and third round of financing, ensure that your books meet the standards of generally accepted accounting principles (GAAP), expand market share, and turn profitable."

You'll have to attract potential acquirers or talk to investment bankers about going public. If a company wishes to buy your company, you'll go through a process of extensive due diligence and evaluation. If you choose to go public in the United States, you'll file Form S-1 with the Securities and Exchange Commission, have a prospectus created, and go on an investor road show to pitch the merits of investing in your company.

Finally, you'll sell part or all of your company—either to an acquirer or to the public markets. Your equity—your ownership—will soon be liquid, and you'll be able to cash in on the past 5 to 10 years of 80-hour workweeks. You might make $5 million or you might make $500 million—depending on the market capitalization of your company and the amount of equity you were able to retain through all the financing rounds and option pool dilutions.

This is how, at the basic level, the system of entrepreneurship works. Going public or selling a company is a dream for many high-potential entrepreneurs.

If you can start with a product that the market demands, raise funding, build a good team, establish market share, turn profitable, add more products and revenue streams, and position yourself as a market leader in your niche, you'll make it. This process is not exactly easy, however, and more often than not, even the most experienced, well-educated, well-connected entrepreneurs fail on this path. It often requires three or four tries, each taking five or more years of an entrepreneur's life, to take a venture public or have a highly successful exit.

> "If you can start with a product that the market demands, raise funding, build a good team, establish market share, turn profitable, add more products and revenue streams, and position yourself as a market leader in your niche, you'll make it."

Which Type of Business to Start?

Let's take a minute to analyze the pros and cons of starting a high-potential and lifestyle business. Lifestyle companies include small consulting companies, local restaurants, laundromats, barbershops, hardware stores, and any kind of franchise. In general, lifestyle businesses are local businesses with sales less than $5 million.

The advantages of starting a lifestyle company include being able to control the company, being able to continue to do what you love without carrying too much risk, having a positive cash flow early on and a relatively constant one thereafter, having to report only to yourself, and being able to take time off whenever you want. Disadvantages include not being able to hire top talent (as talented people usually avoid companies that offer no stock options and only limited opportunities for personal growth) and not having the chance for huge gains.

High-potential companies, in contrast, generally are either developing a product that they will sell internationally, are based on a technological breakthrough or change in regulatory environment, or are raising venture capital to explore a lucrative opportunity. These companies are usually C corporations and, if they succeed, have the possibility of reaching $50 million in annual sales within five to seven years.

The advantages of starting a high-potential company include the possibility for large returns on your investment, the ability to attract outside investment, and the ability to build a great team who will work with you to make your company succeed. Disadvantages include the usual necessity for the company to take on large amounts of debt or lose significant amounts of equity, a loss of control as investors and employees dilute the founder's equity, and the long wait to reach positive cash flow.

On the topic of lifestyle versus high-potential ventures, Harvard Business School researcher Amar Bhide in his *Harvard Business Review* article, "Questions Every Entrepreneur Must Answer," writes:

> The company of a lifestyle entrepreneur does not need to grow very large. A business that becomes too big might prevent the founder from enjoying life or remaining personally involved in the work. In contrast, entrepreneurs seeking capital gains must build companies large enough to support an infrastructure that will not require their day-to-day intervention.

There is surely no right or wrong choice here. You just have to make sure the choice you make synchronizes with your goals. If you are able to take a risk and are shooting for an exit event of $10 million or more, then you will need to start a business that fits within the high-potential category. However, if you are unable or do not wish to take a large risk, or are content making a few hundred thousand dollars a year with the potential for a larger return over an extended period, a lifestyle business may be for you.

To better analyze which option you prefer, take a look at Table 3.1, which lists the key differences between lifestyle and high-potential companies.

Table 3-1 Differences between lifestyle and high potential ventures

Key Difference	Lifestyle Company	High-Potential Venture
Exit strategy	Usually none, sometimes sell through business broker at low earnings multiple.	Strategic acquisition sale to private equity group, or initial public offering (IPO) at a multiple of revenue.
Ownership	Founder is majority owner.	No majority owner; CEO owns 5–30% of company at sale.
Financing	Bootstrapped, organic growth, or self-financed.	Angel investors or venture capitalists for seed round. Additional rounds until cash flow positive or sold.
What is sold	Services or products with low differentiation.	Products with proprietary intellectual property or based on recent changes or new technology or high-margin and value-add services.
Family members	Often part of business.	Infrequently part of business.
Entity Type	Sole proprietorship, partnership, LLC, or S corporation.	C corporation, usually incorporated in Delaware.
Market	Local or regional.	National or international.
Failure rate	High.	Very high.
Founders makes money from	Salary net profits/ dividends.	Liquidity event and sale of equity.
Board of directors	Composed of company members.	Composed of investors, industry leaders, and one or two company heads.

(Continued)

Table 3-1 Differences between lifestyle and high potential ventures (*Continued*)

Key Difference	Lifestyle Company	High-Potential Venture
Systems	Fewer processes or systems. Often make money only while open.	Many processes and systems. Make money even while owners are sleeping or operated around the clock.
International sales	Few	Many. May be international offices and/or manufacturing operations.

Table 3.1 should help you as you align your personal goals with your business goals. On this topic, Amar Bhide continues:

If entrepreneurs find that their businesses, even if very successful, won't satisfy them personally, or if they discover that achieving their personal goals requires them to take more risks and make more sacrifices than they are willing to, they need to reset their goals.

If you have yet to do so, I encourage you to commit your personal goals to writing. Analyze the reasons you wish to start a business. Then take a look at the amount of risk you wish to take at this point in your life and the return you hope to achieve.

How to Get Out of the Middle Class

Let's analyze the key decisions that you must make in life to be on the path toward becoming wealthy. The large majority of people in the developed world work at a job, earn $30,000 to $60,000 per year, and spend nearly all of, if not more than, their incomes each year. At the end of 40 years of working, many of these people must live the last years of their life dependent on Social Security and their 401(k) plan. Many are content with such a life, which is, of course, fine. However, many are not. If you are not, then please read on.

The wealthy, however, build assets, invest in assets, and have their assets work for them. Assets are items that generate positive cash flow. The wealthy certainly are willing to work at a job for a period of time, but the experience and contacts they gain from a position are much more important than the initial salary to them. They gain control over their expenses. The amount of money they save during a year is more important than the salary they earn.

The wealthy put off present consumption and the purchase of luxuries like vacations, boats, and big-screen televisions so they can invest in building an asset that will provide enough passive cash flow to buy 20 vacations, a cruise line, and a big-screen television company in the future. They never go into debt for something that is for pleasure and not investment. They buy things like businesses, securities, options, bonds, and real estate. They intelligently use their businesses to pay many of their expenses, thus receiving numerous tax advantages. They use their expenses to make them richer, and they have no fear of debt, as long as they are using debt to build an asset and not purchase unnecessary items.

The poor often live frugally, not realizing that time is more important than money. The rich realize that time is more valuable than money because with time you can make money, but with money you cannot make time. They understand the principal of opportunity cost and do not hesitate to spend $1,000 for someone to paint their house if during that time they can make $3,000 working at what they do best.

The rich have their money work for them. They do their due diligence and research and invest it in public and private companies, and then sit back while their money makes them more money. They build companies that make them money while they are sleeping. Most mornings they will wake up richer than when they went to bed.

They realize the importance of developing multiple streams of income and creating passive cash flow—money that comes in whether or not they go to work. They stay out of the middle and lower classes by waiting, if possible, until they have consistent passive cash flow from their businesses and investments before they get married and have children.

While the rich may have to start off making money through earned income, they realize the advantages of and focus on building passive income from investments. The rich also know that they cannot become wealthy overnight, and they invest the time, gain the knowledge, make the contacts, and take the actions needed to become successful. The rich keep close track of their cash flow. They have accountants and in the early stages use programs such as QuickBooks, Quicken, and Money to keep track of all of their income and expenses, both personally and in their companies.

> "The rich also know that they cannot become wealthy overnight, and they invest the time, gain the knowledge, make the contacts, and take the actions needed to become successful."

The validity of these principles is made clear to me each and every day in my life. There is a terrible disparity between the rich and the poor, even in the streets of Chapel Hill, North Carolina. Certainly some of this disparity is caused by a lack of equality of opportunity, but some of it exists for reasons other than differences in education and opportunity. Some of this disparity exists because those who are poor were not aware of the principles by which the rich make their money.

Too often, poor people work for others and not for themselves, spend more money than they earn and go into debt for unnecessary items, do not defer present consumption to invest, fail to take the initiative to improve their financial literacy and business education, and get married and have children before they secure a well-paying job, let alone a stream of passive and portfolio income. Don't let your life take this path—and if it already has, learn and apply these principles in everything you do and you will overcome a bad start to make it in the end.

The Secret to Becoming Rich

Robert Kiyosaki and Sharon Lechter state, in *Rich Dad's Guide to Investing*, that the secret to becoming rich is to "build businesses and then have your businesses buy other cash producing assets such as other businesses or real estate." This statement captures the essence of the process required to become extraordinarily wealthy. I would modify this statement slightly, however. I believe the following:

> The secret to becoming extraordinarily wealthy is to build and invest in businesses and then use the excess cash flow from your businesses and the capital gains from any liquidity events to invest in future ventures, early-stage private companies, emerging markets, public securities, and other cash-producing assets such as real estate.

Please reread this statement a few times. This is the path I will follow throughout my life. I am currently in the process of building a successful business. Once this is accomplished and we're able to sell to the private or public markets, I will use the funds to make additional investments in early-stage private companies, build additional companies, invest in real estate, and explore investments in other countries. I intend to make my first $20 million by building companies. I'll hope to earn my next $200 million by investing half my assets in my future businesses, private equity, hedge funds, venture capital, and income-producing real estate, while keeping half my assets allocated in small-cap growth and value stocks and emerging market indexes.

It's important to remember that financial security and financial prosperity should be looked at as a *long-term game*. If you are age 30 and are $40,000 in debt, make a goal to have this debt paid off by 35. Then make a goal to have $200,000 in the bank by 40. Then by 45, to become a millionaire. Take it one step at a time, work with five-year plans, and each day make sure you're working toward your long-term goal. It will become easier and easier as you gain in experience and contacts and as you are able to leverage your existing capital to help create more capital.

If you're young, consider saving up what you can and opening an online trading account with E*Trade or TD Ameritrade. In my experience, the easiest thing to do if you don't want to actively manage your investments is to put your assets in no-load index funds called exchange-traded funds (ETFs).

While I am not qualified to give financial advice and I would certainly recommend consulting a financial advisor, if by age 25 you can get $15,000 into a portfolio that closely matches the market, not touch it until age 65, and let the returns compound, you would have $471,000 after inflation by the time you retire (assuming an average inflation-adjusted annual return of 9 percent). If you can get $15,000 into a similarly structured portfolio by age 25 and commit to putting $1,500 per year into the portfolio, you will have $1,023,000 after inflation by the time you retire. A little sacrifice early on can make a big difference down the road and allow you to feel safer taking larger risks, such as starting your own business, with the other 50 percent of the money you save.

In the Information Age, it is not she who works the hardest that succeeds; it is she who has the best ideas and is able to execute best. While, yes, there still are considerable barriers to entry in many industries, no longer are the poor stuck being poor. With education (in the classroom or not), the right ideas, the courage to take calculated and educated risks, an entrepreneurial spirit, and a bias toward action, almost anyone can become a millionaire and, with a little more of these ingredients, become a billionaire. Wealth has been democratized.

For a History of the market system, check out my essay online at http://www.ryanallis.com/history-of-the-market-system.html.

The Industrial Age paradigm of going to school, getting a secure job, and working hard is very unlikely to make you very rich. MIT economist Lester C. Thurow argues in his book *Building Wealth* that the movement from the Industrial Age to the Information Age has resulted in considerable economic disequilibria, creating the possibility for considerable economic gain.

Within business, many examples exist of the power of ideas. In the mid-1970s a nineteen-year-old by the name of Bill Gates came up with an idea that has made him the wealthiest man in the world: that

for an essay on the dot com crash and the information age, visit www.ryanallis.com/dynamics-of-the-information-age.html.

computers would need software and an operating system. It was a computer company started out of a dorm by Michael Dell that dwarfed the goliath at that time, IBM. How? With simply an idea—the idea to sell personal computers directly to customers instead of through distributors and retailers.

Are You Right for Entrepreneurship?

Being an entrepreneur is not for everyone. Not everyone can handle the stress, risks, and responsibilities of having dozens or hundreds of people's lives depend on your choices or reporting to a board of directors or panel of your investors. An analysis of the traits commonly found among successful entrepreneurs might assist you in deciding if you are right for the role of entrepreneur.

Here is a list of commonly noted traits of entrepreneurs. Put a check next to each one you believe you have.

__ Initiative	__ Drive toward efficiency
__ Bias toward action	__ Ability to take feedback
__ Vision	__ Tolerance for stress
__ Determination	__ Decisiveness
__ Courage	__ Ability to deal with failure
__ Creativity	__ Ability to learn from mistakes
__ Perseverance and persistence	__ Ability to delay gratification
__ Drive to achieve	__ Ability to plan

__ Orientation toward opportunity

__ Ability to build a team

__ Ability to prioritize

__ Ability to deal with the abstract and ambiguity

__ Ability to inspire and lead

Do you possess these attributes? If you checked more than half, you may have what it takes to become a successful entrepreneur.

As part of a series of interviews I conducted for this book with six successful entrepreneurs in North Carolina, I asked the question, "What traits are most important for an aspiring entrepreneur to have?" I gave the entrepreneurs 15 options and asked them to number their choices 1 through 15 in order of importance. The results were very interesting. The most important trait for aspiring entrepreneurs to have, according to these five successful entrepreneurs, was "being able to build a solid team." The second and third most important skills were "leadership and the ability to inspire" and "persistence." The least important attribute of all, number 15, was "a college degree." Here are the full results in order of importance:

1. Being able to build a solid team
2. Leadership and the ability to inspire
3. Persistence
4. Motivation and ambition
5. Integrity
6. Ability to communicate effectively
7. Confidence
8. Being able to execute
9. Having a bias toward action
10. Having a good idea or plan
11. Knowledge of marketing
12. Good networking skills
13. Having the right advisors
14. Knowledge of accounting and finance
15. A college degree

Would you work 70-hour-plus weeks for months on end; sleep at the office when you get backed up; put your own money on the line when payroll is due and the bank has yet to approve a loan; be the janitor, the receptionist, the customer support representative, the bookkeeper, as well as the president; and get up and present in

> "Would you work 70-hour-plus weeks for months on end, sleep at the office when you get backed up, and put your own money on the line when payroll is due and the bank has yet to approve a loan?"

front of a room of investors after already being turned down by 50 other banks, angel investors, and venture capital firms? If you think so, then you just might have what it takes to become a successful entrepreneur.

There is no successful entrepreneur who would say building a successful company is easy, and there is no one who would say that there is no risk involved in building a company. If building a company were easy, there were no risk, and it did not take years of dedication and persistence, everyone would be an entrepreneur. Unfortunately, the market has little compassion. It doesn't pull for the person who works the hardest or the person who has the best idea. It pulls for the person who works the most in-

For information on the best and worst things about being an entrepreneur, check out my essay available at www.zeromillion .com/young/best-worst- entrepreneur.html.

telligently, sells what the market demands, puts together the needed resources, gets deals done, and executes.

In the next chapter, we'll take a look at what motivates entrepreneurs. What is it, exactly, that makes them work 70-hour weeks, wake up after five hours of sleep six days per week, and risk their savings and their livelihoods for their dreams?

4

STEP 2: FIND YOUR CORE MOTIVATION

★

If you're alive, there's a purpose for your life.

—PASTOR RICK WARREN

The second step in building a successful company is to determine your core motivation. Figuring out the reasons why—why you want to spend the next few years of your life building a company—is absolutely critical to your eventual success.

It takes at least five—and maybe seven or ten—years to build a successful company. If you are going to spend this much of your life, not to mention your money, sweat, tears, and reputational equity on building an organization, know why. Know that you have a strong reason to get up every day, a reason so strong that you will be passionate each day of your life about it. It must get you out of bed, and it must inspire you to make sacrifices.

When deciding on the type of company you want to build, you'll have to take a close look at your personal goals. Do you want to attain a certain lifestyle, gain respect, create an innovative product, build an organization that will outlive you, contribute to your community, have an outlet for your talent, or be free from your job?

> "Do you want to attain a certain lifestyle, gain respect, create an innovative product, build an organization that will outlive you, contribute to your community, have an outlet for your talent, or be free from your job?"

What are the reasons that you wish to start your business? Do you want to become extraordinarily wealthy, increase efficiency in an industry, have enough income to provide a comfortable life for your family, or travel the world as you grow your firm?

Take time to write down these reasons. I'd caution you about building your business without first aligning your business plan with your personal goals. If you don't love what you do, it is very difficult to give it your all.

An entrepreneur's personal and business goals are closely linked. Unlike the manager of a public company who has a fiduciary responsibility to maximize value for shareholders, as the founder of a company you have some ability to build your businesses to fulfill personal goals. If you are unsure what these goals are, take out a pen and paper and write down every reason you have for starting a business and what your personal goals are.

> "If you can align what you love with what you do and what you do with what you're passionate about, you will be so much more successful in life and in business."

Ask yourself, will I be passionate about going after this goal? If you can align what you love with what you do and what you do with what you're passionate about, you will be so much more successful in life and in business—however you define success for yourself.

So ask yourself, "What is it that will motivate me to be willing to spend the next few years of my life shaping my vision into a thriving organization?"

There can be many motivations. It is rarely one thing that motivates dedicated action within an individual. You could have a desire *to do* something or a desire *for* something.

Action Item 1: Know Your Motivations and Goals

Write down every reason you have for starting a business and what your goals are for the business:

_____

_____

_____

_____

_____

_____

_____

_____

What Motivates You?

You could have a desire:

- To create a great product
- To create jobs
- To play the game
- To change an industry
- To help your customers
- To change the world
- For influence
- For recognition
- For respect
- For money

What's on Your Epitaph?

Here's a thinking exercise that can help you determine your core motivation. Let's assume for a moment that reincarnation does not happen and you have only one life to live. Now think, what words do you want to have on your gravestone? What do you want your epitaph to say? Let's assume you have four lines of up to 35 characters each. Here's an example:

Great Woman, Wife, and Mother	29 characters
Entrepreneur and Humanitarian	29 characters
Changed the World on a Global Scale	35 characters
Fought Poverty through Love	27 characters

By starting with the end in mind, you can ensure that what you are planning on doing today and for the next few years will enable you to create the opportunities that allow you to fulfill your highest ambitions. At your funeral, how will those closest to you describe you? What will you have done? What will your accomplishments be? And what plans and direction should your life take to enable you to get to the point at which you can truly achieve great success.

Action Item 2: Start with the End in Mind

Take a moment to write down your preference for your four-line epitaph:

_____

_____

_____

_____

One day your life will be done. And in your place you will have left something. What will that something be? How will you be remembered? What impact will you make? What will you create that continues on after you are gone?

> "One day your life will be done. And in your place you will have left something. What will that something be?"

Why I Am an Entrepreneur

So why have I have chosen to do what I do? There are six reasons:

1. I love the game.
2. I like being able to provide jobs.
3. I enjoy giving back to the local community.
4. I enjoy creating something that helps people.
5. I like being financially secure.
6. I'm passionate about changing the world on a global scale.

I love to play the game of business. It is really what gets my blood going. I am a very competitive person, and I am passionate about entrepreneurship. I am glad we have competition, for it is competition that drives me. I have a desire to be the best.

At iContact and Virante, we've created over 90 jobs in the past five years, and we have the ability to create hundreds more in the next five years. We contribute to the support of 41 children. Between our team members' spouses and their children, we help support over 170 people every month through our efforts so far.

At times, having responsibility for and supporting so many people can weigh on you. It's a really big responsibility, though it is something that drives me. It's something that gives me a reason to get up each and every day and work the hardest I can to create something that is truly worthwhile.

We are able to give back to our community by sponsoring organizations such as Nourish International, the Full Belly Project, AGRADU, Junior Achievement of Eastern North Carolina, Orange County Foster Care, the Chapel Hill–Carrboro Chamber of Commerce, Durham County Habitat for Humanity, and the Debian Project.

In terms of creating a product that helps people, I very much enjoy being part of a team that is developing an application that enables over 20,000 other businesses and 100,000 individuals to more easily communicate online.

I enjoy the opportunities, experiences, and positive influence that come along with having financial freedom. There are a few ways to make a good deal of money in this country and in the world. I could be a professional athlete, I could be a white rapper, I could make my way up the corporate ladder, or I could start my own business. Starting my own business is the path I chose for myself.

When I went into this business I had $12,000 to my name, and that was being depleted at the rate of about $1,000 a month. I realized I had about 12 months to be able to make this thing work. My original salary was $50,000, but we didn't have any money and we couldn't pay it. So we accrued that salary until September 2004, when we finally had enough to pay ourselves something.

From the beginning we knew that we weren't doing it for the money. That's not the reason we do business. We see money, cash flow, and profits as the lifeblood of our organization, not the purpose of it. We strive for them only because they are essential in fulfilling our true mission of creating jobs, creating a great product, and creating a great organization.

> "[At iContact,] we see money, cash flow, and profits as the lifeblood of our organization, not the purpose of it. We strive for them only because they are essential in fulfilling our true mission of creating jobs, creating a great product, and creating a great organization."

Today we are doing well, and if we are fortunate enough to go public or sell to a strategic acquirer, I may be financially secure for the rest of my life, which will allow me to focus my time and efforts on my true passion: reducing global poverty and changing the world through entrepreneurship, social entrepreneurship, and politics.

My true passion in life is working to reduce poverty in developing nations. Entrepreneurship is the best way I know to gain money and influence now so I can give back in a larger way later through social entrepreneurship, public service, and philanthropy.

The motivation is the result of a realization I had when I was 17. When I was 15, I had gone through a phase of rebellion. I had red hair; I was into punk rock music. I didn't understand what the purpose of life was. I really didn't comprehend how I, as an individual, could make a difference in this world. This got me down. I was in a rut.

With the support and the help of my parents and some of my teachers, and as a consequence of some of the experiences I had had, I was able to emerge from that phase in my life and by age 17, I had become a person who was very motivated to get up every day.

There were also three books I read at that age that changed the direction of my life and got me out of that rut once and for all. The first book, *Rich Dad Poor Dad,* by Robert Kiyosaki, taught me about financial freedom, how to build assets, and how to structure companies. The second, *Think and Grow Rich,* by Napoleon Hill, originally written in 1928, gave me a personal philosophy centered around positive thinking, goals, and appreciation for life. The third, *The Lexus and the Olive Tree,* by Thomas Friedman, opened my eyes to globalization and how the world worked, and inspired my love for economics and reducing poverty through business, health care, education, and effective governance.

My Core Motivation

There are two facts that really disturb me and motivate me to do my best every single day so that I can work to change the realities these facts describe in the future:

1. 2.7 billion people in our world, 42 percent of the world's population, live on under $2 a day.
2. 49,345 people (the majority of whom are children) die every day in developing countries from preventable diseases and starvation.

"2.7 billion people live on under $2 per day, and 49,345 people die every day in developing countries from preventable diseases and starvation."

Once you know these two facts, you cannot pretend that you do not know. When I came across similar statistics in books like *The End of Poverty*, by Jeffrey Sachs, it added meaning, focus, and dedication to the pursuit of my goals. Knowing that our generation, for the first time in human history, has the real opportunity to end the final travesties of mankind captivates and inspires me.

Ensuring a sustainable environment and reducing poverty, malnutrition, and hunger while improving access to health care, education, and opportunity are the issues I am truly passionate about and what I hope to work on over the next seven decades of my life through business entrepreneurship, social entrepreneurship, public policy, and politics.

I have been fortunate enough to find my core motivation, which drives me every day to be excellent in everything I do. It is driving me to write these words now. It drives all that I do, and all that I strive for. Finding this core motivation before I started iContact at age 18 has been critical to getting me through the difficult and challenging times and finding the strength from within to persevere in the face of otherwise insurmountable odds.

Spend time thinking and meditating on your raison d'être, your reason for being, and figure out what constitutes the core motivations for what you do and who you are. Know who you want to become, and you can begin to direct your life rather than letting outside factors control you. Direct your life toward your definite chief aim. Let who you are and what you believe come out in all that you create.

5

STEP 3: EVALUATE YOUR IDEA

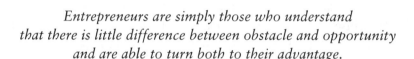

*Entrepreneurs are simply those who understand
that there is little difference between obstacle and opportunity
and are able to turn both to their advantage.*

—NICCOLO MACHIAVELLI, FIFTEENTH- AND SIXTEENTH-CENTURY
ITALIAN STATESMAN

Deciding on What to Sell

Before you can start a company, you must decide on what you will sell and how you will make your money. Experienced entrepreneurs often have a number of business ideas that, given the time, they would like to pursue. As an aspiring entrepreneur, you might not have an idea yet.

If this is the case, you'll have to develop an idea or partner with another aspiring entrepreneur who does have one. Business ideas tend to develop in entrepreneurs' heads over the course of years, often while they are working at a regular job. Almost always, business ideas are refined and modified as time passes and more knowledge is acquired and research done.

When I taught entrepreneurship to high schoolers at the Lead America conference in Chicago and Boston a few summers ago, each team of participants had to come up with a number of business ideas and then, over the course of a few hours, narrow the list to two ideas, for which the team would create full business plans. We began by filling the walls with blank poster paper and just letting the students shout out what came to their minds. You can do a similar exercise.

During a brainstorming session, write down whatever comes to mind, or focus on a specific industry in which you have experience. Think about the products you use every day and how they could be better. Think about a business you interact with and what you would improve if it was your business. Think about things that you would love to have if they existed. Consider the efficiency of the marketplace and attempt to find inefficient and bloated industries that you could enter. Think about whether you would rather provide a service or sell a product. Consider the possibility of buying into a preexisting franchise. Consider what you are good at and what people would pay you to do for them. Consider macro trends in the economy such as the aging population and the advent of the Internet.

Although idea brainstorming can be a helpful activity, the best ideas are often not generated as a result of this process. More frequently, they come through experience in an industry, from people

Action Item 3: Business Idea Brainstorm

Take a moment to write down any business ideas you have, including a description of the product or service and the market you will sell to.

_____

_____

_____

_____

you know, or from a moment of inspiration. Don't be discouraged if you cannot come up with any ideas that you want to start a business around. It takes time. In the meantime, make sure you are always looking for opportunities and networking with as many people and at as many events as you can.

Here are four tips for coming up with business ideas:

1. *Continually be aware* of the products you use everyday. How might they be improved? What need or pain do you have that could be fulfilled or remedied by a product or service that is not currently being provided?
2. *Go to networking events,* seminars, and conferences. You might find someone with a good product or a good idea who is looking for partners. Read magazines and publications that cover the industry you are interested in.
3. *Intern or get a job at a company in the industry* you are interested in. Work there to get experience and build contacts. Many times you will see product ideas in the course of your work that your company chooses not to pursue.
4. *Find a partner* with a business idea whom you can join up with.

It's important to remember that opportunities are created when there are changing circumstances. Whenever you experience new things or the world around you is changing, there will always be lots of opportunities. If you are lacking in ideas, you also may wish to ask around about internships that are available at local entrepreneurial companies or apply for a job at one. Working at an entrepreneurial company with other entrepreneurially minded people is one of the best ways to come up with new business ideas.

If you work at a larger company, I'd suggest talking with your manager to see if there are any new products or technologies the company is developing. By expressing interest in coordinating the development and launch of a new product, you may just get a promotion to being a manager with profit-and-loss (P&L) responsibil-

ity for that product—allowing you to be an intrapreneur and leverage company resources while you build the new segment of your
company.

How to Evaluate Your Idea

Once you are able to come up with a potential business ideas, the
issue arises of determining whether your idea is a true business opportunity. One of the best ways to determine the potential of an idea
is to screen it through an opportunity evaluation model.

Opportunities are simply good ideas. When an idea is timely, attractive, achievable, durable, fills a need, and provides value to the
buyer, it can be considered an opportunity. An idea is an opportunity
only if there is reason to believe the market will validate the idea and
the management team has the ability to execute the idea. Let's take
a look at an opportunity evaluation model and see how our business
ideas stack up.

The MAR Model of Opportunity Evaluation

In analyzing your ideas to decide on the one that you will select for
your business plan, you must be able to administer a test to determine whether they truly are valid opportunities. I created the Market, Advantages, Return (MAR) Model to provide a screen through
which you can pass your business ideas to see if they are genuine opportunities with a demonstrated need, ready market, and the ability to provide a solid return on investment.

> All achievements, all earned riches, have their beginning in an idea.
>
> **—Napoleon Hill**

Is the idea feasible in the mar-
ketplace? Is there demand? Can it be executed? Are you able to assemble the people and resources to pull it off before the window of
opportunity closes? All of these questions must be considered and
answered.

To determine whether your idea has a good chance of being validated in the marketplace, it must be analyzed based on a number of criteria. You must look at the need, market structure, pricing, market size, timing, cost structure, barriers to entry, intellectual property, the team, distribution channel, profitability, time to breakeven, needed investment, exit strategies, and return on investment.

Let's take these terms and turn them into an easy model that you can use to evaluate the business ideas you've come up with or your current business venture.

M—The Market

1. *The need.* This is one of the most important questions to ask. Is there a big need for this product or service? Try to avoid ideas that sound novel or unique but for which there is no real market. Make sure your product or service fills a need or solves a problem. Also make sure there is demand for the product or service in the location(s) where you will be selling or providing it.
2. *Market structure.* Is the market a highly competitive market or more like an oligopolistic or monopolistic market? Determining the number and quality of competitors and type of market is important when developing your strategy to enter that market and determining the needed investment.
3. *Pricing.* What will you charge? Will there be a high enough markup? Is there enough demand in the marketplace to justify the price you intend to charge? What are your competitors charging? Settling on a price that is not too low to be unprofitable but not too high to drive away the majority of your buyers can be a hard task.
4. *Market size.* Is the market big enough to warrant entry? Is it growing or shrinking? Look for a growing market that will become of significant size.
5. *Timing.* Is the market ready for your product? You may have a great idea for flying cars, but if consumers are not ready for

your product or the prerequisite infrastructure is not in place, you may not be able to turn your idea into a successful business.

A—The Advantages

1. *Cost structure.* Who will your suppliers be? What will each element of your product(s) cost to source or manufacture? If you can find a way to have lower costs than your competitors, you'll improve your profit margins and have a big advantage.

2. *Barriers to entry.* Are there large competitors in the market niche? Are there regulations, patents, or large capital requirements that will get in your way? If there are many barriers to entry, it will be difficult to enter a market.

3. *Intellectual property.* Do you have a proprietary advantage such as patents or exclusive licenses on what you will be selling? If so, you'll have an easier time raising funding and, if your technology is good, the chance to build a very successful company.

4. *The team.* Who can and will you bring on to help build your company? Will they be offered equity? How many people will you need to get the company off the ground, and what will be their roles? If you can convince an industry veteran to join your board or an experienced vice president, chief operating officer (COO), chief technology officer (CTO), or chief financial officer (CFO) to join your team, you'll have a big advantage. Remember, if the management team does not have the ability to execute the idea, it is not a true opportunity.

5. *Distribution channels.* How will you be selling your product? Will you sell it directly to consumers via the Internet, sell it to wholesalers, sell it to businesses, sell it to retail stores, or sell through a network of partners? If you

can develop a unique and efficient distribution channel, you will surely have an advantage.

R—The Return

1. *Profitability.* Will your company make a positive net income? Will your revenues eventually be higher than your expenses? If not, either take a second look at your projections or try another idea.
2. *Time to breakeven.* Based on your projections, how long will it be before the company is cash flow positive? How long will it be until the company begins to have an aggregate net income and reaches cumulative breakeven? These are figures to know and two very important graphs to have in your business plan.
3. *Investment needed.* How much money will it take to start up this venture? Will it be $20,000, $200,000, or $2 million? The amount of money you need will give you an idea of where to go to raise funding. For under $50,000, friends and family and the bank are your best options. For $50,000 to $1 million, accredited private investors, partner companies, and angel investors are likely your best bet. Above $1 million, you'll have to look to venture capital firms or other companies that are willing to provide start-up capital for you. Do your best to minimize the amount of capital required to start the business. If you are able, start with only your personal resources. Once you have revenues, you will be able to raise investment funding much more easily and without having to give up as much.
4. *Exit strategy.* Do you plan to sell the company or go public down the line? How will your investors get their money back? If you do not plan to ever sell your company or go public, you will not be able to raise equity capital.

5. *Return on investment (ROI).* What is the return for your investors based on your current projections? If it is not high enough, you won't be able to raise certain types of capital. Venture capitalists look for at least a 5× return over five years or less, with a target of closer to 10×. This is not to say that you should make your projections higher. Rather, you may wish to explore alternative ideas, look at the possibility of taking less money at a lower premoney valuation, or look at alternative financing such as angel investors and debt capital.

Table 5.1 summarizes the MAR model for opportunity evaluation. Once entrepreneurs have gone through this opportunity evaluation model, they are able to proceed with the venture—with the opportunity—in an informed way, confident that their idea will be validated in the marketplace.

So how does your idea stack up? Based on your answers from this screening process, do you consider it to be a true opportunity? Is there a demonstrated need, a ready market, and the ability to provide a solid return on investment? If you believe so, congratulations! If not, I encourage you to follow the tips given earlier for generating and finding additional ideas and opportunities. Then proceed with the MAR Model.

Table 5.1 MAR model for evaluating new ventures

Market	Advantages	Return
Need	Cost structure	Profitability
Market structure	Barriers to entry	Time to breakeven
Pricing	Intellectual property	Investment needed
Market size	The team	Exit strategy
Timing	Distribution channels	Return on investment

The 10 Axioms of Opportunity

I'd like to share with you the 10 Principles of Opportunity. I developed these principles while writing a speech that I presented to a group of high school students in Chicago in June 2003. These axioms will help you determine when an idea is a good opportunity, as well as what one must know in order to create good opportunities.

> The vitality of thought is in adventure. Ideas won't keep. Something must be done about them.
>
> **—Alfred North Whitehead**

1. An idea is an opportunity when it is timely, attractive, achievable, durable, fills a need, and provides value to the buyer. An idea is an opportunity only if there is reason to believe the market will validate the idea and the management team has the ability to execute the idea.
2. To be a true opportunity, a business idea must have a demonstrated need, a ready market, and the ability to provide a solid return on investment.
3. Opportunity-focused entrepreneurs and investors start with the customer and the market in mind. They analyze the market to determine industry issues, market structure, market size, growth rate, market capacity, attainable market share, cost structure, the core economics, exit strategy issues, time to breakeven, opportunity costs, and barriers to entry.
4. Business ideas are a dime a dozen. What really matters is the execution and the quality of the team. It is not the idea. It is the people and their ability to execute that matter. Once you have the people and the execution, then your idea has the potential to become a true opportunity.
5. Too many people wait for opportunities to come to them. Don't wait for the opportunities to come to you. Create the opportunity for yourself.

Action Item 4: Use the MAR Model to Vet Your Idea

Take a moment to evaluate your idea using the MAR Model to determine whether it is a true business opportunity.

Market

What is the need for the product or service?

_____

What is the market structure?

_____

How will I price the product?

_____

What is the approximate size of the market?

_____

Is the market ready for the product?

_____

Advantages

What will it cost to produce your product or service?

_____

What is the total start-up cost?

_____

Will you need to acquire or protect any intellectual property?

_____

Who will be on your team?

_____

Will you sell your product to businesses or consumers?

_____

Return

What will your gross profit and net profit margins be based on your projections?

_____

How long will it take to reach breakeven and at what unit production level will breakeven be reached?

_____

How much money does the company need to get to cash flow positive comfortably?

_____

What is my exit strategy? Do I intend to sell the company, go public, or make money off of quarterly profits?

_____

If my projections are correct, what can an investor expect to make for an investment in my company and what will be the payback period? Will the investor make money through dividends or a liquidity event?

_____

6. If you are not ready for an opportunity during the short window in which it exists, it will pass you by. You must make personal development a priority so that you will be prepared to take advantage of the opportunities.

7. Every adversity comes with a seed of equal or greater benefit. Through adversity, opportunity will come.

8. The world is filled with opportunities just waiting to be found by an energetic and intelligent person.

9. Making mistakes, learning from them, and being willing to put yourself out there are essential to finding opportunities.
10. With a positive mental attitude, a desire to succeed, a determined mindset, persistence, and enthusiasm, you can find, create, and take advantage of any possibility and any opportunity that you can dream of.

Why So Many Businesses Fail

According to a longitudinal study conducted by the U.S. Small Business Administration (SBA), approximately 60 percent of small businesses shut down within the first six years. Small businesses fail for numerous reasons. The eight most common reasons new businesses fail are that their owners:

1. Grow their company too fast
2. Have a poor concept
3. Are not good at marketing or sales
4. Fail to plan
5. Start their company without enough money to get to breakeven
6. Have an inability to differentiate
7. Lack control of their finances and books
8. Don't build systems and processes

Many entrepreneurs who end up unsuccessful do not build processes and systems and lack the ability or desire to sell. They do not carefully plan their business and often fail to raise the needed capital to sustain it until it is profitable. They do not focus on efficiency of operations or automation. They never make the investment in additional capital or employees needed to expand the company to the point where it can make a profit. As an entrepreneur, even if you have a great idea, you will have to plan well, build a good team, make sure you have adequate capitalization, build the proper systems, and execute your plan.

According to Colin Wahl, entrepreneur and adjunct business professor at UNC's Kenan-Flagler Business School, there are certain critical success factors in building a successful small business. These include:

- Vision of the management
- Passion
- A good idea
- Clean, focused business objectives
- A well-thought-through business plan
- Good organizational design
- Persistence
- Determination
- Strong work ethic
- Enthusiasm in the owners
- A good team
- Motivated employees
- Good cash flow management
- Adequate financial resources
- A clear understanding of market need
- Execution of the management

As you can see from this list, a good idea is only one of many factors necessary for success. Ideas are a dime a dozen. Unless you have a Ph.D. and are doing cutting-edge research at a top university, if you have thought of a business idea, someone else has thought of it, too. The key to success, then, is rarely the idea and is nearly always good execution. To illustrate this principle, let's take an example.

In 1967, an angel investor, Fred Adler, received over 50 business plans from entrepreneurs who proposed to start microcomputer firms. Only one of the teams presenting this idea ever made it: Data General. But why did so many entre-

"It is not the idea, it is the people and their ability to execute that matter."

preneurs pitching plans to sell microcomputers fail to receive funding or, if they were funded, never succeed?

They didn't make it not because their ideas were bad per se or because they didn't have the potential to be good opportunities. They were great ideas and enormous opportunities. Rather, they failed because their entrepreneurial teams were unable to execute.

A Note for Entrepreneurs in Developing Countries

If you live in a developing country, it may be more difficult for you to start your business. Many of the steps listed here for starting and building a business may be different in your country. If you are in a less developed country, you may not be able to easily access capital, and the incorporation process might be entirely different. The business infrastructure could be in a less developed condition, there might be corruption in some elements of the company registration process, and you may be asked to pay bribes to obtain the needed permits. If this is the case for you, please know that I hope to spend much of my life working to make the opportunity to start a business available to anyone, anywhere.

If you are from a developing country and run into difficulties, I encourage you to continue as an entrepreneur, to learn about sources of microcredit and assistance organizations, and to work to remove corruption and build the infrastructure necessary for innovation and progress in your country.

I encourage you to put pressure on your government to follow the work of people such as Peruvian economist Hernando de Soto. It is my hope, however, that many of the general steps in this book will still be applicable and that within my lifetime it will be possible for people of all nations to have equality of opportunity and the freedom to express their creativity and passion through commercial and social entrepreneurship.

Recall the dot-com era of a few years ago. Many of these companies had good ideas, but they were lacking in terms of execution. I have heard many venture capitalists say they would rather have an A management team and a B business concept than an A business concept and a B management team. It is not the idea, it is the people and their ability to execute that matter. While a business that ends up being successful could be started with a so-so idea, a successful business will never be built without a good team.

By making sure you screen your ideas through the MAR Model of Opportunity Evaluation, you can get a good idea of whether they constitute true opportunities. But as you can see, execution is just as important as, if not more important than, the idea. So let's look at how to plan for your business and then execute based on that plan.

6

STEP 4: WRITE YOUR PLAN

★

If you fail to plan, you plan to fail.

—THOMAS JEFFERSON, THIRD PRESIDENT
OF THE UNITED STATES

The Business Plan

Until September 2003, I had never written a full-fledged business plan. I always planned informally, in the form of one-page check-lists or handwritten sales forecasts. Although we had operational plans and marketing plans, we didn't have a full business plan. I had never attempted to raise significant capital, and thus never needed a plan.

In early September 2003, I met with a potential board member for iContact. In reviewing the company, he asked to see our business plan. I said I would send it to him. That weekend I sat down and wrote for about 12 hours, finishing it off with executive biographies, a 15-page marketing plan, projected organizational charts, and a projected (pro forma) income statement.

Although you will not need a business plan per se until you are ready to raise funding, it is good to have one right from the beginning. Writing the iContact business plan allowed me to take a step back from the day-to-day operations of the company and look at where we were, both financially and in the timeline of executing our strategies, and where I wanted us to go over the next two years.

It was especially helpful to take the time to write down all our current and projected expenses. It helped me determine whether we needed to raise additional funding or if we would be able to grow organically as a result of cash flow from operations. The pro forma pinpointed the exact month, based on my current knowledge of every expense and revenue source, in which we would turn cash flow positive and the exact month in which we would reach cumulative breakeven.

If your idea is sufficiently developed that you are ready to start a business around it, I'd suggest writing a business plan for it. Your plan should not be a static document; rather, it should be a lively, dynamic work that changes and grows as your business grows. In your plan, you should include the following basic elements.

Executive Summary

The executive summary is a quick overview of all elements of the business plan, highlighting what exactly it is you will sell, how you are different from your competitors, why your team will succeed, how much money you'll need to launch the business, and what the expected return on investment will be for investors, based on your projections. Here is the actual iContact Executive Summary from June 2007 that we used to raise $5.35 million.

The Team

In the team section, explain who you are and who will be helping you build your business. What is their background and experience? Who else will come on board once you launch and/or receive funding? Why will your team fit together well? Who will be needed as your business expands? You should include an organizational chart of what you envision your firm looking like in a year and then a few years down the road. As an example, Figure 6.1 shows the iContact org

iContact Executive Summary, June 2007.

Overview: iContact Corp. is a Durham, NC SaaS provider in the online communications space. Founded in July 2003 by serial entrepreneurs Ryan Allis and Aaron Houghton, the company has grown to 57 employees and an annual run-rate of over $6.3 million. The company's mission is to be the leading worldwide provider of on-demand software that makes online communications easy.

Financing: iContact was bootstrapped by its founders until May 2006, when it raised $500,000 in convertible debt from investor NC IDEA. The company has increased its monthly sales from $180,000 to $530,000 since the close of this round. The company has successfully identified highly profitable channels of customer acquisition that it can scale with additional funding. iContact is seeking to raise $3 million to $5 million in expansion capital in Q3 2007.

Products: The company has two product offerings: iContact and iContact Enterprise. iContact makes it amazingly easy to create, publish and track email newsletters, surveys, autoresponders, blogs, and RSS feeds. As of June 2007, iContact has over 11,000 paying customers including market leaders like Vonage, Symantec, Century 21, Ford, Nissan, International Paper, Bank of America, Intuit, Re/Max, Centex Homes, and United Colors of Benetton. These and the thousands of other iContact clients generate over $530,000 in monthly recurring revenue.

Management: iContact has a world-class and fully built-out rockstar team—from a pair of serial entrepreneur founders who intimately know the market, to a technologist and marketer who are leaders in their fields, to a VP of Business Development with over 30 years of experience, to a CFO who helped raise over $100 million in the public markets for Broadband Technologies public in 1996, was the CFO for

(Continued)

iContact Executive Summary, June 2007. (*Continued*)

OpenSite—sold to Siebel in 2000 for $550 million in one of North Carolina's largest software company acquisitions, and was most recently CFO of CipherTrust in Atlanta, which sold for $270 million.

Customer Acquisition: The average iContact customer pays $50 per month and stays around for 24 months, creating a lifetime value of $1,200. The team has identified scalable methods of acquiring customers at a highly profitable customer acquisition cost, and has scaled its new customer acquisition rates from 300 to over 1100 new customers per month since July 2006. The company has over 1,300 Channel Partners.

Strategy: iContact is leveraging the base product to create the future of online communication, by creating a single central platform for businesses to manage all of their online communications. As RSS becomes mainstream during 2007, iContact is positioned as the easiest method of publishing content to a feed.

Vision: iContact's vision is to become the worldwide leader in on-demand software that makes communication easy by combining principles of the Software as a Service (SaaS) model with the web 2.0 trends of user-generated content and community engagement. The company is developing the first platform that makes online communication really easy for the masses.

Address:
2635 Meridian Parkway, 2nd Floor
Durham, NC 27713

Key Team Members:
Aaron Houghton, Chairman, Co-Founder, and Chief Innovation Officer
Ryan P. Allis, CEO and Co-Founder
Timothy K. Oakley, CFO

David Rasch, CTO
David Roth, VP Business Dev.
Brandon Milford, VP Marketing
Chuck Hester, Director of Corp. Comm.
Cindy Hays, Director of Human Resources
Amber Neill, Director of Customer Service
Robert Plumley, Director of Financial Operations

Number of Employees: 57
Bank: Bank of America
Law Firm: Smith Anderson
Auditor: Hughes Pittman & Gupton
Current Investor: NC IDEA
Board Structure: Ryan Allis, Aaron Houghton, Merrette Moore
  (NC IDEA)
Capital Raised to Date: $500,000 (5/06)
Financing Sought: $5M

Use of Funds:
Rapid scaling of customer acquisition for fully developed product

Key Points:
1. Rapidly growing 57- person company with 11,000 customers and $510,000 in recurring monthly sales.
2. Identified highly profitable customer acquisition model that is scalable with additional investment.
3. Company bootstrapped until $500k convertible debt round in May 2006.
4. Grew sales from $176,000/month to $510,000/month since last round.
5. Sustainable unique technological advantages that allow low-cost scalable technical structure.
6. Rockstar team with significant IPO, acquisition, and market experience.

(Continued)

iContact Executive Summary, June 2007. *(Continued)*

7. Working toward becoming worldwide leader in on-demand software for online communication.

Financial Summary, Historical

	2003 Actual	2004 Actual	2005 Actual	2006 Actual
Revenue	$11,964	$297,794	$1,314,136	$2,900,683

Reprinted with permission from iContact.

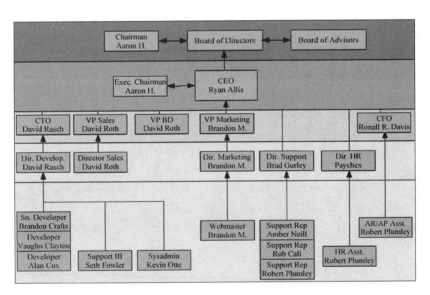

Figure 6.1 iContact organizational chart.

chart from when the company had 15 employees (some people fill multiple positions).

Product or Service

What is it that you sell? What differentiates your product or service from those of all your competitors? What unique technology/intellectual property, if any, do you have? How does the product work?

Market

Who are your competitors? What strengths and weaknesses do they have? What is the size of your market? Is it growing? What share of the market can you reasonably capture?

Marketing and Sales Plan

How will you position yourself in the marketplace? What is your distribution strategy? Who is your target customer? What strategies will you use to make sales and build awareness of your company?

Challenges and Risks

What are the problems you might run into? What are the potential challenges you will face, and how will you deal with these? What world events or competitors or government actions might impact your business? What are the risks?

Capital Use

How much money are you seeking (if any) and how will the funds be used? For product development? Buying hardware? Customer acquisition? Building a sales team? Explain how you will use investor funds.

Pro Forma Financial Projections

Create a full projected income statement, monthly through year two, and then quarterly for years three through five. Here is the procedure for doing this:

1. Start by listing all the categories for your current expenses and those in the future.
2. Fill out the actual dollar figures for any data to date and projections for the future, month by month for year one and quarterly through year five.
3. Project your sales volume and revenues for each of your revenue streams.
4. Subtract your monthly expenses from your monthly revenue to determine how much money you will lose or earn in each month. This is called your *net monthly income.*
5. Find the point where this number turns from negative to positive. That point is when you will have reached cash flow positive.
6. Below the net monthly income row, create a cumulative net income row in which you add up all the prior monthly (or quarterly) net incomes.
7. Find the point in this row where the number is the greatest to the negative side. This is the amount of money you will need, at minimum, to start your business, based on your projections.
8. To be safe, double this amount and make it your goal for how much money you need to raise to start your business.
9. Find the point where your cumulative net income turns positive. This point is called *cumulative breakeven.*
10. Finally, create a break-even analysis graph similar to the one that appears later in this section to illustrate the time and money needed until your company turns profitable.

So you can visualize what your expenses might look like, Table 6.1 shows the actual projected expenses for the first six months of iContact.

Table 6.1—Pro forma expenses for first six months of iContact

	Jul	Aug	Sep	Oct	Nov	Dec
Hosting	150	150	150	150	150	150
Servers	0	0	0	0	0	1000
Salaries	0	0	0	0	750	1000
Legal	0	1547	0	0	0	0
Rent	0	0	200	200	200	200
Phone	50	50	80	90	130	130
Computers	0	0	480	0	0	500
Internet	0	0	0	0	0	0
Furniture	0	0	0	0	0	0
Advertising	0	0	0	0	0	100
Utilities	50	50	50	0	0	0
Commissions	0	0	0	77	43	125
Office supplies	50	50	50	80	80	150
Parking	80	80	98	160	160	240
Travel	0	0	0	0	0	200
Meals	0	0	20	50	50	100
Printing	0	0	20	50	100	100
Security	0	0	0	0	150	0
Merchant acct.	0	0	0	20	33	65
Gateway	0	0	250	20	30	30
Total	380	1927	1398	897	1876	4090

So you can see what the projections for a more developed company would look like, Table 6.2 shows the projected expenses for iContact in months 19 through 24.

Putting the revenue projections and your expense projections together, you'll have your pro forma income statement. Table 6.3

Table 6.2—Pro forma expenses for iContact during months 19–24

	Jan	Feb	Mar	Apr	May	Jun
Hosting	1000	1150	1150	1300	1300	1450
Servers	1000	1000	1000	1000	1000	1000
Salaries	15000	18000	21000	24000	27000	30000
Legal	300	400	400	400	400	400
Rent	2000	2000	2000	2000	2000	2000
Phone	500	500	500	500	500	500
Computers	0	500	500	500	500	500
Internet	70	70	70	70	70	70
Furniture	200	200	200	200	200	200
Advertising	10000	10000	10000	10000	10000	10000
Utilities	200	200	200	200	200	200
Commissions	9500	10500	11500	12500	13500	14500
Office supplies	200	200	200	200	200	200
Parking	560	640	720	800	880	960
Travel	1200	1200	1200	1200	1200	1200
Meals	500	500	500	500	500	500
Printing	200	200	200	200	200	200
Security	300	300	300	300	300	300
Merchant acct.	2730	2990	3250	3510	3770	4030
Gateway	30	30	30	30	30	30
Total	45490	50580	54920	59410	63750	68240

shows the pro forma income statement for the first seven months of iContact.

Note the available cash line, where we kept track of how much money we had left in our bank account, assuming a starting investment of $5,000. It declined to $1,955 by October, and then started to grow as we began to make more money than we spent.

Table 6.3—Pro forma for first seven months of iContact

	Jul	Aug	Sep	Oct	Nov	Dec	Jan
Revenue	261	771	432	1250	2500	4250	7500
Expenses	380	1927	1398	897	1876	4090	4101
Net income	(119)	(1,156)	(966)	353	624	160	3,400
Aggregate net income	(923)	(2,079)	(3,045)	(2,692)	(2,068)	(1,908)	1,492
Available cash	4196	4077	2921	1955	2308	2932	3092

The next thing you will need to do is create a break-even chart to graphically show when you turn cash flow positive and when you reach breakeven. Figure 6.2 is the actual initial break-even chart for iContact (we later went back into the red when we raised investment so that we could grow faster).

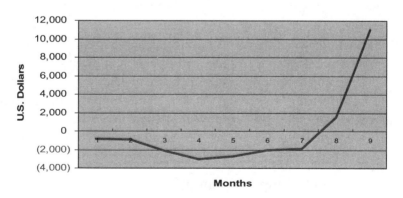

Break-Even Analysis: Aggregate Net Income Months 1-9

Figure 6.2 Break-even chart for iContact.

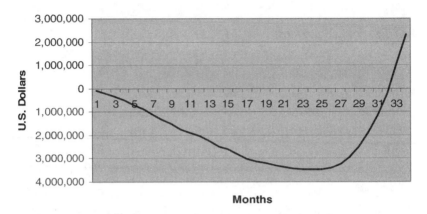

Months

Figure 6.3 Typical break-even chart for a successful venture-capital-financed technology venture.

As you can see, the company went about $3,000 in the red before it turned cash flow positive. We were using our own funds to grow the business. Had we been a traditional venture-backed company, we would have had a much larger initial loss. A typical break-even chart for a successful venture-capital-financed technology venture might look like Figure 6.3.

Once you have your business plan completed, if you are in the United States you may wish to schedule an appointment with the local chapter of the Service Corps of Retired Executives (SCORE, www .score.org). They'll review your plan with you and provide feedback. If you know any business owners or successful entrepreneurs, invite them to lunch and ask for feedback on your plan. To protect yourself, if you do show your business plan to anyone you do not know well, be sure to have them sign a confidentiality and noncompete agreement. Do note that venture capitalists and most investors will not sign these. However, you are protected by the industry ethic.

Creating a Mission Statement

Once you have your business plan in place, there is just one more element of organizational planning to complete. It is very important to create a common mission statement for your business that all your team members can agree to and get behind.

As a new company owner, especially if there is more than one person working in the business, writing the mission statement might be one of the most important things you can do. Often partners will have rather different ideas about the direction and strategy of a company. By answering the 10 questions in the following list collaboratively and creating one document that everyone involved in the company agrees to and signs, you will not only minimize headaches and arguments down the road but your goals will also be fully aligned, enabling you to work together efficiently.

The iContact mission statement encapsulates the overarching goal that we are attempting to accomplish for the organization. It reads:

> iContact's mission is to be the worldwide leading provider of on-demand software that makes online communication easy.

We also have a longer mission statement that we call the iContact Manifesto, which resides on our Web site and speaks to the reasons we are in business, our general strategy and positioning, who are customers are, the philosophy behind what we've built, an explanation of what we are trying to accomplish, and how we intend to be part of our community.

Mission statements can be short or they can be long, up to several pages. You may wish to come up with both a short mission statement that you'll show to all your customers and promote and a longer statement for internal guidance and planning.

Examples of short mission statements include the following:

Avis: Our business is renting cars. Our mission is complete customer satisfaction.

Eastman Kodak: To be the world's best in chemicals and electronic imaging.

McDonald's: To offer the fast food customer food prepared in the same high quality manner worldwide, tasty and reasonably priced, delivered in a consistent, low-key décor and friendly atmosphere.

If you plan to write a longer mission statement, simply answer the following 10 questions.

10 Questions Your Longer-Version Mission Statement Can Answer

1. What problem(s) do you solve? What need(s) do you fulfill?
2. What do you sell? How do you make your money? What is your revenue model?
3. How are you unique from everyone else out there? What is your unique selling proposition?
4. Whom will you sell to? What is your target market?
5. What are your economic/financial goals?
6. What are your social/community goals?
7. What type of company do you want to create? Will you build a lifestyle company or a high-potential company?
8. Where is the company going? What products/services/industries do you plan to venture into?
9. What is your five-year strategy? Do you want to sell internationally, build an online store, franchise your business, build certain partnerships, or develop additional products?
10. Do you ever plan on selling the company or going public? What is your exit strategy?

It may take weeks, multiple meetings, and some editing to create a single document that everyone will sign. Although it takes time to prepare, I cannot overemphasize the importance of having such a document. Not only does it dramatically reduce conflict and prevent arguments, but it also aligns everyone in your business with the same goals, in turn creating a much more effective team and much more profitable business.

Creating a Corporate Values Statement

Twice a year we hold an iContact Day with all of our team members at an off-site location, usually at a hotel on a Saturday morning and afternoon. At the first iContact Day in January 2006, we developed our company's Corporate Values Statement. This statement brings together the key principles we intend to follow as we attempt to accomplish our mission. Our Corporate Values Statement reads as follows:

Corporate Values Statement

iContact's mission is to be the worldwide leading provider of on-demand software that makes online communication easy. While our mission is what we strive for, how we achieve the goal that it represents is just as important. With this in mind, we have established this Corporate Values Statement to serve as a reference for us and those that come after us. In fulfilling our company mission, we will strive to always:

1. *Value People First:* We will respect and value our customers—for it is they who allow us to survive and prosper. We will communicate openly with our customers, keep them in mind when making business decisions, and provide them with a high level of service and assistance.
2. *Build People Up:* We will respect and value each team member and work to build people up through positive reinforcement in a caring family environment. We will understand that mistakes are okay, as long as they are learned from.
3. *Be Competitive:* We will maintain a strong competitive ethic. We will strive to reach our goals by building a superior team, developing innovative products, and providing clear unique value propositions to our clients. We will work to keep sales high and expenses low, although we will always choose to invest for long-term benefit in both the company and our people.
4. *Be Innovative:* We will always be thinking about how we can improve what we're doing, what is coming next, and how we can create what is next in our markets.
5. *Be Quick Yet Thorough:* We will have a bias toward action, yet maintain standards of quality and excellence in all that we do.

(Continued)

Corporate Values Statement (*Continued*)

6. *Have a Culture of Responsibility:* We will work together in collaboration with our team members and draw on the experience, skills, and knowledge of all to progress toward our goals. When we see a ball that may drop, we will do what it takes to pick it up and assist other members of our team.
7. *Work Hard, Have Fun:* We will always work hard and choose to go the extra mile when needed. In the same sense we will always remember to enjoy ourselves and keep our environment fun, dynamic, and energetic.
8. *Give Back:* As we succeed, we will give back in kind to organizations in our community, region, nation, and world that strengthen our society, provide resources that help us succeed, or help those in need.

Spend some time and thought developing your corporate values statement in conjunction with the other members of your team. The effects of a team driven by a higher mission can be truly revolutionary.

The Different Types of Businesses

There are many different types of businesses that you can start. All, however, will fall into one or more of the four basic categories: manufacturing, wholesale, retail, or service. A manufacturing business actually make the products, wholesale businesses sell the products to stores, and retail businesses sell the products to end buyers—which may be businesses or consumers. Service providers, on the other hand, sell their time and expertise rather than a tangible product.

My experience in business is in selling products wholesale and retail and providing a service. In my experience, I have found that there is a very big difference between running a product-centered company and running a service-centered business. My product-centered business is called iContact. We sell Web-based e-mail marketing and blogging software. My current service-centered business is called Virante. Virante provides Web marketing consulting services for high-potential companies and takes payment in cash, equity, and commissions on generated sales.

Whether you start a service-based or a product-based business will in large part impact on the steps you'll have to take to build it to $1 million in sales. I find that product businesses, in general, have a higher potential and are easier to grow exponentially, whereas service-based businesses are nearly always limited.

When you are selling a product, you can make money while you're sleeping; however, in most service-based businesses, you can make money only when you're working. Your income is limited by the number of hours you can work. In order to overcome this handicap, service-based business owners need to put the proper systems and processes in place and hire employees who can do the work for them so all they have to do is manage the company and set its vision.

> "To reach that $1 million level in sales, you'll have to stop working in your company and start working *on* your company."

You'll have to find high-margin services in areas where you can genuinely add value for your customer. While services such as programming, Web design, marketing consulting, and search engine optimization can be lucrative, it is rare that a one-person company makes more than $200,000 per year. To reach that $1 million level in sales, you'll have to stop working in your company and start working *on* your company—the classic advice of Michael Gerber, in his book *The E-Myth*.

Another difference I often find between product- and service-based companies is that there is often only one founder of a service-based business, whereas there are more often than not three or four founders of a product-based company. This holds true with my companies. I maintain 100 percent of the ownership of Virante, Inc., but share the ownership in iContact with 11 others.

I consider iContact to be a high-potential company that I hope will sell for hundreds of millions of dollars in a few years, while Virante is a service firm, holding company, and tax-advantaged business. This is further evidenced by the fact that iContact is a C corporation—as most large corporations are—whereas Virante is an S corporation, allowing the profits of the company to pass through without being taxed twice.

When your company sells a product, you can automate much more of the business—especially if that product is delivered online or you can set up an autobilling system. You can easily automate an affiliate program, shopping cart, and online merchant account—and then hire someone at $15 per hour to do the shipping and answer the phone. In addition, there is much more capability to scale.

If you do decide to start a service-based company, see whether you can also develop a product based on your expertise in your niche—perhaps an e-book or informational product. If you can develop a product in addition to your services, you'll acquire extra credibility and be able to develop a stream of income that will allow you to increase your revenue in a way that is not directly tied to the number of hours you work.

Robert Kiyosaki and Sharon Lechter offer a good illustration of this concept when they note the difference between a small, self-employed service provider and a business owner, in their book *Rich Dad's Guide to Investing*:

> Those who are self-employed will never become rich because they are not building an asset. If they stop working, they will stop making money. If a business owner stops working, he or she will continue to earn passive income from the asset he has built. At the core of assets are systems.

Entity Selection

To form your company, you'll first need to decide which type of entity to become. In the United States, you can choose to be a sole proprietorship, partnership, limited liability company (LLC), S corporation, or C corporation. There are different advantages and disadvantages to each depending on what your business will be doing and what your eventual goals are for the company.

A corporation is a legal entity whose personality and rights are separate from those of the collection of individual members it represents. The rights of a corporation include being able to sue, hold assets, hire employees and contractors, enter into contracts, and make bylaws that govern its activities. A corporation's general purpose is to develop and sell products and services and maximize the value of the organization for its shareholders.

It is generally accepted that Nevada is a good state in which to incorporate for low taxes and privacy; Delaware is a good state in which to incorporate if you intend to raise investment funding or sell your company, as it has business-favorable laws and an extensive case history, and most corporate lawyers are familiar with Delaware law. Any U.S. resident can incorporate a company in any state he or she chooses. Before you incorporate, you should speak to a corporate attorney to get advice and recommendations.

When you incorporate, you can do it yourself, with the assistance of an online incorporation mill, or with a lawyer. It will cost about $200 to do it yourself, $300 online, and $1,500 through a lawyer, and perhaps a bit more if your company has more than one founder. In all, iContact paid our original law firm, Hutchinson & Mason, approximately $3,000 for incorporation and all the start-up formalities. It was worth every penny, however, as we had six different initial shareholders and a complicated capitalization table and vesting options.

To incorporate a company yourself, you'll simply need to know the name of the company, the number of shares you wish to create, and the state in which you wish to incorporate. Once incorporated, you will receive your Articles of Incorporation from the state attorney's office and a set of bylaws and stock certificates. After this, contact the IRS to get an Employee Identification Number (so you can open a bank account and hire employees), choose whether to continue as a C corporation or file Form 2553 to elect to be an S corporation, and hold your first board meeting.

I ended up meeting the iContact attorney through the Legal Issues for High Technology Start-ups MBA class I took in the spring of 2003. If you do choose to go with a lawyer for incorporation and do not already know whom to choose, inquire about the following when evaluating each of the law firms you are considering:

- Reputation and references
- Experience with start-ups/expertise (have they done this before?)
- Introduction to angel network
- Access to venture capital firms
- Library of precedents (firm has library of documents used before)
- Potential employees/board members
- Contacts in industry

Contracts and Agreements

When you launch your company, there are certain documents that you will need in order to protect your idea and follow the proper regulations. In forming iContact, there were over 33 different documents that we had to execute among the five initial shareholders in order to launch the company. When forming your company, make sure you have all founders, independent contractors, and employees sign a nondisclosure, confidentiality, and noncompete agreement. All consultants will need to sign a consulting agreement, and all employees will need to sign an employment agreement. You should also have a stock restriction agreement for all those receiving stock that has yet to vest.

Securing Your Intellectual Property

Intellectual property (IP) consists of all the intangible assets of your company. These can be trademarks, trade secrets, copyrights, or patents. In the United States, the U.S. Patent and Trademark Office (USPTO) is the organization with which you will have to file a record

Important Documents for Start-up Companies

Nondisclosure agreement: This is the initial document to be signed before any discussion of work commences. It prohibits the signer from passing on any information he or she learned that is deemed confidential.

Confidentiality and Noncompete agreement: This is a more comprehensive agreement that supersedes the original nondisclosure agreement. It also contains a noncompete agreement with a provision that the signer cannot join or start any company in your industry for at least one year after his or her termination of the relationship with the company.

Employment agreement: This should be signed by all new employees. It sets the salary, benefits, term, and scope of employment.

Consulting agreement: This should be signed by all new independent contractors. It sets the wage, term, and scope of the consulting relationship.

Stock restriction agreement: This is for all those who will be receiving stock that has yet to vest. It sets the terms under which the person may obtain and sell shares.

of your IP. An overview of the major types of IP is provided here for your convenience.

Copyright

A copyright is the right to govern the use of creative works and obtain the economic benefits from the use of such works. You can copyright computer code, images, books, works of art, or any original works of authorship. However, you can copyright only the tangible expression of the work, not an idea behind such work. While the act of creation gives copyright, you can receive additional rights if you register a copyright with the U.S. Patent and Trademark Office. In the United States, copyrights last 70 years after death for an individual.

Trademarks ^(TM) and Service Marks ^(SM)

If you have created a company or product name, you may wish to protect it with a trademark. You can trademark slogans (e.g., "Where do you want to go today?"), letters that constitute an abbreviation (e.g., HP), symbols (e.g., logos), and sounds (e.g., the Apple Macintosh start-up sound). You can register a trademark with either a state or the federal government. To obtain protection throughout the United States, however, you should register with the U.S. Patent and Trademark Office. The USPTO bases its decision to grant a trademark on distinctiveness and whether you are in the same industry as holders of similar trademarks. Once you receive your trademark, no one else can use that trademark without your permission. You can also file for a service mark if there is a special name for a service you provide. If you are in the United States, you can file for a trademark yourself at www.uspto .gov or use your law firm. The fee is $335 for a trademark.

Patents

Holding a patent can give a business a significant advantage over its competitors and be a big plus for potential investors. Patents give the right to a person or entity to be the only one that does something in a certain way. Most often it is new inventions or new processes that are patented. To be eligible to receive a patent, the idea or invention has to be novel and nonobvious. Obtaining a patent is not cheap, however. It usually costs between $10,000 and $15,000 and usually takes 18 to 24 months to be approved. Once you do receive a patent, you have the right to be the only one to use your idea for 17 years. In exchange for the patent rights, however, you have to make public the methods you used to create the process or invention.

Trade Secrets

One problem with a patent is that after your 17-year protection period, anybody can use your idea. Because you have to explain the idea in detail when you file and these records are made public, a patent often does not offer the lasting protection a company needs. Consequently, a trade secret can often be a better option than a patent, as a trade secret never expires. A classic example of a trade secret is the Coca-Cola formula.

In order to protect a trade secret, there must be a high level of security. All employees must be compelled to sign confidentiality and nondisclosure agreements, and information should be provided only on a need-to-know basis. Such protection is essential, as once a trade secret gets out, it is no longer a trade secret.

While it is important to protect your key trade secrets, consider carefully what you are willing to share. Corporate transparency is generally appreciated by customers and allows you to get more media coverage, build a more passionate

> "Corporate transparency is generally appreciated by customers and allows you to get more media coverage, build a more passionate user base, and generate more buzz about your company."

user base, and generate more buzz about your company. This book is an example of a company's willingness to maintain transparency in order to reap the benefits of word of mouth and openness within a culture of bloggers for which the era of one-way megaphonic communication is clearly over.

Protecting Your IP

In order to protect your intellectual property, make sure you have all employees and contractors sign a nondisclosure, noncompete, confidentiality, and assignment of invention agreement before they start work. Make clear what is confidential information by always marking it with the word "Confidential." Also, when an employee leaves, be sure to hold a debriefing session to remind the employee of his or her responsibility to not reveal your trade secrets and confidential information.

Now that we've looked at how to write a business plan, let's move on to determining the required start-up capital for a business and look at methods of raising money.

7

STEP 5: RAISE FUNDING OR BOOTSTRAP

He who will not economize will have to agonize.

—Confucius

Once you've found a good business opportunity or developed a good product and have incorporated, you may need some money to get off the ground. Depending on the scope of your plans, you may be able to afford to launch the company through self-financing. In other situations, you may need to raise a few thousand dollars from friends and family, apply for a $25,000 loan from your bank, raise $250,000 from angel investors, or bring in $3 million from a seed-stage venture capital firm. Your experience, sophistication, current revenue level, market size, location, relationships, competitive differentiation, and team will determine your ability to raise funds.

If you do need to raise money, you'll first need a good business plan. Once this is done, take a look at your pro forma financial statement and identify the cumulative shortfall before you begin to turn cash flow positive. A good rule of thumb is to double this number, and then make this amount your goal for the amount of money you need to raise.

Table 7.1 Where to find the money

If you're looking for	You'll most likely get it from
$1,000 to $25,000	Friends, family, your contacts, bank loans
$25,000 to $250,000	Angel investors, bank in some cases
$250,000 to $1 million	Group of angel investors, Small VC firms
$1 million+	Venture capital firms

There are two types of capital that you can raise for your company: debt capital and equity capital. *Debt capital* basically consists of loans you have to pay back with interest, whereas *equity capital* consists of investments for which you provide partial ownership in your company.

Table 7.1 summarizes the places to find capital based on how much you are seeking.

Debt versus Equity

While staying with my brother at his apartment in Queens in March 2003, I had the opportunity to talk to one of his roommates by the name of Mitch. After finishing a dinner consisting of an authentic New York City mushroom and cheese pizza, Mitch and I started talking about the business he wanted to start. He told me about his idea, the market knowledge he had gained so far, and how he hoped to bring his product to market. He also mentioned that he would need funding for the venture and asked for some advice on how to obtain it. "I hope to obtain venture capital, but am not positive how it works," Mitch stated. "Do I sell them 49 percent of the company for their investment? What will be the valuation for the company if there aren't any sales yet? Should I go to a bank first?"

I explained to Mitch that while I had not yet raised venture capital myself, I had raised money from private investors for one of my companies, taken an MBA class on venture capital deal structure, and participated in the Venture Capital Investment Competition at UNC's Kenan-Flagler Business School.

I provided Mitch with an overview of the different types of capital available to an early-stage venture and how he might go about obtaining each. The following information is essentially what Mitch and I discussed that night.

Nearly every type of funding falls into one of two categories—debt or equity. Debt has to be paid back (it is a loan), whereas equity funding does not. In exchange for equity funding, the investor receives a percentage ownership (shares) in your company that grows proportionally with the overall value of your company. At a liquidity-producing event such as a sale of the company or an initial public offering (IPO) to the stock markets, the equity holders could cash out their stock, ideally receiving a large return for taking the risk early on.

In his article "Financing Instruments," attorney Michael T. Redmond explains the difference between debt and equity:

> Although there are certain exceptions, debt instruments generally represent fixed obligations to repay a specific amount at a specified date in the future, together with interest. In contrast, equity instruments generally represent ownership interests entitled to dividend payments, when declared, but with no specific right to a return on capital.

Debt Financing

Standard types of *debt* (the word is a shortened form of *debentures*) include personal loans from family members and friends, bank loans, issued notes, venture debt, accounts receivable loans (called *factoring*), and corporate bonds. These financing loans are provided at an agreed-upon interest rate and time period. Some debts, called convertible debts, can be converted to common stock later on, but most are paid back with cash on a set schedule or set date. Other types of debt, such as venture debt, have interest accruing until the end of the maturity date, with the upside provided to the lending firm (such as

Silicon Valley Bank or Square One Bank) through options to purchase shares in the company.

Whether the receiver of the loan pays only the interest during the term of the loan and the entire principle (the initial amount of the loan) back at the end, or pays part of both the interest and the principle at each payment period, is specified in the terms of the loan. Debt instruments can be secured by assets of the corporation or personal assets, or by organizations such as the Small Business Administration, or they can be unsecured (backed by a pledge of credit or equity in the company).

The advantages of providing debt capital to a business include a reduction in risk, since upon bankruptcy debts must be paid back before any assets can be distributed to stockholders, and a good chance of receiving the initial principle with interest back within a set period of time. Disadvantages for the issuing institution or person include not being able to participate in the value growth of the company in most cases.

The advantages to a business of taking debt capital include having less dilution and raising money at an effectively lower cost. Venture investors generally require target annual returns of at least 35 percent, compared to between 5 percent and 15 percent for debt capital (depending on the current prime rate, your willingness to secure the loan, and the risk perceived by the lender).

There are many types and structures of debt. The box that follows reviews a few of the more common forms.

Obtaining funding can be a difficult process, but there are a few things you can do to increase your chances. Here are some tips:

- If you are seeking only a few hundred or a few thousand dollars, you should first look to friends and family and then to the banks. If you have assets to back it up (such as cash in your bank account, a house, or a car), you should be able to obtain a loan with relative ease.
- If you do not have an adequate credit history or assets to back up the loan, the bank may ask you to find someone (such as a parent or friend who does have adequate assets) to cosign the

The Different Types of Debt

Friends and family loans: These are loans from your friends and family, generally on favorable terms. Be careful taking money from your friends and family—it can make Thanksgivings a bit harrowing! iContact took a $5,000 loan from a friend of ours to help us purchase server equipment early on.

Corporate credit cards: Many entrepreneurs use credit cards to finance their ventures early on. iContact presently has two credit cards with a $100,000 and a $60,000 line of credit, respectively. Credit cards generally have a much higher interest rate, in the neighborhood of 12 to 19 percent, than credit lines.

Personally secured loans: These loans to your company are secured by personal assets such as real estate.

Corporate secured loans: These loans to your company are secured by company assets such as accounts receivable, inventory, company real estate, or machines.

SBA-backed loans: These loans to your company are secured in part by the U.S. Small Business Administration. iContact was able to obtain a $10,000 credit line (later expanded to $29,600 and $133,000) backed by the SBA. Our bank, Bank of America, was willing to provide us with a credit line equal to 10 percent of our prior year's revenue.

Convertible debt: These loans to your company convert into debt after a period of time. iContact raised $500,000 as convertible debt from local venture capital firm NC IDEA (later converting into equity in their IDEA Fund).

Venture debt: These are loans to your company from a venture debt firm such as Square One Bank or Silicon Valley Bank. iContact utilizes a $1 million line of credit (LOC) from Square One Bank. Normally, these firms are willing to lend an amount equal to your last two months' revenues—but generally only after you raise venture capital from an established institution. They also often take warrants (essentially the same thing as options to

(Continued)

purchase equity at current fair market value) to increase their upside.

Corporate bonds: Later on in the life of a company, when it is making millions of dollars in annual sales, it can set its own terms by putting together a memorandum and selling bonds to the public or private markets. The company will set the length and interest rate and then attempt to sell the debt instrument. Corporate debt is rated with letter grades based on risk by companies such as Moody's and Standard & Poor's. The higher the perceived risk, the higher the interest rate the company will have to pay.

loan. Remember, the less risk the bank thinks it has, the greater the chance you have of being approved.

- If you have an existing account, a good credit history and credit score, and a relationship at a local bank, the process may not be any more complicated than meeting with a loan officer, discussing your plans, filling out a short form, and waiting a week for approval. However, if you have not established these relationships and history, now is a good time to start.

- If you are serious about raising more than a few thousand dollars of funding, you'll need at least some form of business plan. The more funding you are trying to raise, the more professional and complete this plan will need to be. At its core, you'll need to explain what you will be providing, what need or gap it fills in the marketplace, who you will be working with and who is on your team, your plan for making sales and marketing, and your financial projections including the time to breakeven. You may want to read some of the articles on developing a business plan on www.zeromillion.com for additional guidance or obtain a book on how to craft your plan.

- In general, you will be more successful obtaining financing if you have formed an entity (LLC or corporation) for your business. While it may still be possible to obtain a loan for your sole proprietorship, you will be taken more seriously and have many more avenues open to you as a corporation or other type of limited liability company.

- If you are under 18, you will generally have to have a parent or guardian cosign the loan. You should still be able to obtain a personal loan, provided you have a well-thought-out plan, an established relationship, and assets to back it up, or parents, relatives, or friends who are willing to cosign and secure the loan with assets of their own. If you can learn the language, talk in terms of the bank's interest, reduce risk where possible, and show you have a grasp of accounting and general business knowledge, you very well may be able to obtain the loan you need.
- In the United States, another way to increase your chances of having your loan approved is to go to the Small Business Administration. If you can have your loan backed by the SBA, and, hence, by the federal government, it will be fairly easy to have your loan approved. One of the ways iContact was able to grow early on was through a $10,000 line of credit that the SBA backed.
- When applying for a loan, especially one for a larger amount or one intended to finance a large investment or expansion, be prepared to meet with the loan officers and underwriters for your bank. In short, expect to be drilled from every angle by these persons, and have your answers ready. It is the underwriter's job to reduce risk, so expect hard questions.
- In general if you are looking for U.S. $1,000 to $50,000 in debt funding, a bank should be able to help you. With the right relationships and assurances, you may be able to raise more and at better terms. If you are looking to raise more than U.S. $25,000 (and aren't willing to take out a home equity loan) you may wish to look into equity financing.

Equity Financing

Equity financing provides stock to the investor in exchange for funds. This is usually the form of investment that venture capital funds, angel investors, or other private equity funds make. In exchange for the investment, the investor can benefit from the growth of the company and receive either common or preferred stock.

Here is how you calculate percentages after an equity investment:

Current value of company (premoney valuation):	$40,000
Investment amount:	$10,000
Percent you own after investment:	80 percent
Percent investor owns after investment:	20 percent

Common Stock

Common stock is the most basic form of equity instrument. It represents an ownership in the corporation and includes an interest in earnings. Holders are also entitled to receive dividends (periodic disbursements to shareholders) based on earnings and the decisions of the board of directors.

Depending on the company's or partnership's bylaws or charter, holders of common stock have the best opportunity to share in the company's growth, but also must take into account the increased risk of coming after holders of debt and preferred stock in the case of company failure and bankruptcy.

In the view of the business owner, there is one important advantage to issuing common stock in exchange for financing. There is no obligation to repay the amount invested. The investor's prime reward for taking the risk is participating in the value growth of the company and cashing out upon a liquidity event. Another advantage for the investor is the ability to vote for directors.

Preferred Stock

Preferred stock is a second form of equity. Although it is equity, it can have certain features that resemble debt, which can make it attractive.

Most important to the investor, preferred stock has rights over common stock, reducing the risk of loss of investment. When preferred stock is issued, investors can also negotiate with the company on whether it will be voting or nonvoting stock and how dividends will be distributed. In short, it offers greater flexibility and reduced risk; hence, it is preferred over common stock.

Preferred stock is usually the type of stock issued to venture capital funds upon investment in a company. Usually, the preferred stock will convert into common stock at a 1:1 ratio upon a private sale or public offering.

Equity funding tends to be a totally different ball game than debt financing and generally requires a greater level of sophistication to make it work. If you are looking for equity funding between U.S. $25,000 and U.S. $1 million, you should start by looking at individual angel investors or networks of angel investors. Angel investors are high-net-worth individuals and accredited investors (as defined by the Securities and Exchange Commission) who are able to invest relatively large amounts of money in risky ventures with a potential for a high return.

To attract these types of investors, you will need to have the right advisors (lawyers and accountants with the proper experience and contacts) and have an idea or business that truly has the potential for a high return ($50 million and up, depending on the amount of funding needed).

To increase your chances of being funded, be sure you have a solid business plan, experienced advisors, and a team with market knowledge that has proven it can execute.

Venture Capital

If you are looking to raise U.S. $500,000 and up and you have a business in the technology, biotechnology, energy, or consumer goods space with a potential return greater than $50 million over five years, you may want to look into venture capital funding. At the seed stage (very early stage funding), you may be able to raise between $500,000 and $10 million (or potentially more if it is the right plan with the right people) in a Series A offering of your company's stock. To raise this amount of money and still maintain a good portion of ownership in your company, you'll need to have a high valuation before you accept the funding (your premoney valuation).

For example, if based on your intellectual property, unique idea, and experienced management team, your business was given a pre-money valuation of $10 million and provided with $5 million in Series A venture funding, you will have given away 33 percent of your company.

To increase your chances of being funded by a venture capital firm, be sure you are introduced to the firm by someone they know. This includes entrepreneurs they have previously funded, investors with whom they have done a deal in the past, or an attorney with whom they have worked. Avoid sending in an "unreferred plan."

> "To increase your chances of being funded by a venture capital firm, be sure you are introduced to the firm by someone they know."

Most VC firms receive thousands of business plans per year and can give only a cursory (five-minute) look at most. If you can have a lawyer who works closely with the firm or a successful CEO who worked with the firm in the past introduce you to the targeted investor in person or via e-mail, you'll have a much better chance of getting in the door. When evaluating whether to invest, VCs generally look at the entrepreneurial leadership, the ability of a company to attract talent, and relevant industry experience of the team, as well as looking for a marketing and sales orientation.

In summary, it can be difficult to obtain funding for your business as an aspiring entrepreneur. Many times you'll have to present to dozens of banks and investors before you can find someone willing to fund you. Other times, you'll have to bootstrap the company and grow it organically as your sales grow.

Eventually, around the time your company passes the $1 million mark in annual sales, associates from venture firms will start calling you! It was a great surprise to me in the summer of 2005 when I got my first cold call from an associate at a venture firm. These associates, many of whom already have MBA degrees, work hard to drive qualified deal flow for their partners so that they can become firm partners themselves a few years down the line.

The Seed Round

iContact first began the process of seeking venture capital in the fall of 2005. We had bootstrapped the company since the beginning, using our own funds, a small loan and credit line, and reinvested company sales to build revenue. A friend of mine by the name Jud Bowman encouraged me to consider this path while I was having lunch with him in July 2005 at the local entrepreneurs' hangout, Doce, near our office. Jud is three years older than I and the co-founder and general manager of the leading wireless content software provider Motricity—so I considered his advice seriously and agreed to have him connect me with a few local firms with which he had connections.

The venture firms that we initially spoke to were Wakefield Group, Massey Burch, Southern Capitol Ventures, Aurora Funds, Intersouth, and NC IDEA. We received term sheets from Aurora Funds and NC IDEA; Wakefield Group, Massey Burch, Southern Capitol Ventures, and Intersouth passed. Intersouth and Southern Capitol Ventures came close to providing a term sheet. My friend Jason Caplain, at Southern Capitol Ventures, tells me that he regrets to this day that he did not invest in us early on. Although we are doing very well now, it remains to be seen whether we will be able to successfully exit. Jason is cheering for us regardless.

Initially, we were seeking $250,000 in funding. We talked to Southern Capitol Ventures in November 2005, and they indicated they might be willing to provide this amount at a $3 million valuation. This was much lower than what we were seeking, so we continued our search.

By February 2006 we were in a position to receive a term sheet from Aurora Funds at a valuation closer to what we were seeking, but we were unable to agree on some of the terms—such as founder revesting of shares, liquidation preference, option pool size, and board control—so we passed once again. It was very beneficial that we were cash flow positive as a company at this point, allowing us great flexibility.

It was not until May 2006 that we received a term sheet that gave us the valuation we were seeking at terms acceptable to us. We closed on a round of $500,000 convertible debt from Durham-based non-profit venture capital firm NC IDEA on May 17, 2006. The funds came to us in two traunches, $250,000 up front and $250,000 at the end of the one-year period at maturity with an acceptable interest rate. On May 17, 2007, the debt converted into equity according to an agreed-upon formula, and we were officially a venture-backed company.

The Series A Round

By the time the NC IDEA investment converted into equity, we had already begun raising our next round of funding. Between the May 2006 funding and the time the funds converted into equity, we had increased sales from $176,000 to over $510,000 and our employee count from 22 to 55. We were a much larger company and now had an annual revenue run rate of over $6 million. We were playing a whole different ball game now, and the venture firms were seeking us out.

We presented at three venture conferences in the spring of 2007: the Southeast Venture Conference in Raleigh, the AEA Venture Forum in Atlanta, and the CED Venture 2007 conference in Durham. In all, we had discussions with 39 firms during the process, including NC IDEA, Southern Capitol Ventures, Intersouth, Aurora Funds, Wakefield Group, Frontier Capital, River Cities Capital, Bessemer Venture Partners, Pequot Capital, Scale Venture Partners, Noro-Moseley, HIG Partners, Core Capital, Valhalla, JMI Equity, Novak Biddle, New World Ventures, Capital Resource Partners, Battery Ventures, Growth Capital Group, OCA Ventures, Symphony Technology Group, Edison Venture Fund, Summit Partners, Tudor Ventures, Open View Partners, True Venture Partners, Harbert Venture Partners, Ticonderoga Partners, Highland Capital Partners, Ballast Point Ventures, WWC Capital, Antares, General Catalyst Partners, MK

Capital, Vantage Point, and the private equity groups Kayne Anderson, Alta Communications, and Housatonic Partners.

It became difficult to stay in touch with all of the firms. I did use the help of our CFO, Tim Oakley, when I could, although he was occupied with finishing our annual audit until the last three weeks of the process, when we had to narrow it down to the six firms that we were most interested in. At the end of the day, it was the venture firm that built the most rapport with us, introduced us to partners as well as associates, was willing to follow up and seek us out, saw us for who we were becoming rather than who we had been in the past, understood what we were trying to accomplish, gave us the valuation and key terms we were looking for, moved the most efficiently, and were nice enough to come to see us at our office that got the deal.

> "At the end of the day, it was the venture firm that saw us for who we were becoming rather than who we had been in the past that got the deal."

After a competitive process, we accepted a term sheet from Updata Partners out of Reston, Virginia, a firm with deep operational experience in the software as a service (SaaS) space in which we were competing. We closed on a $5.35 million round on June 30, 2007, providing enough capital for us to continue to expand at a rapid pace and really shoot for becoming a public company or having a $100 million or higher exit. Simultaneously, we accepted a term sheet for a $1 million line of credit from Durham-based venture debt firm Square One Bank. We are, to date, unsure whether we will need or want to raise additional capital in the future. The possibility certainly does exist that we will choose to raise a Series B round in 2008 or 2009.

We will, of course, see what the end result is. We are attempting to grow as quickly as possible now while staying within the sights of profitability. We are taking more risk than before to have the opportunity for a bigger exit and the ability to create more jobs and give back in a more meaningful way to our community and the world. We shall see what the final result will be. It could be $500 million, or it could be nothing at all. Such is the chance venture-backed entrepreneurs often choose to take in our fast-paced, high-stakes, dynamic, competitive economy.

If we can reach at least $40 million in annual revenues and profitability, we will likely be able to file our S-1 and take the company public, probably on the NASDAQ, AMEX, or NYSE ARCA. If we at least have a moderate exit and help our investors make money, we will be able to raise money whenever we need to in the future. In our market system, the more money we can make for others and the more jobs we create in our community, the more we will be able to reinvest and continue the positive cycle of innovation and job creation.

We feel comfortable that with real revenues and a world-class technology, and the expansion of private equity buyouts and alternate stock exchanges, we will be able to have some form of positive exit. We are well aware, however, that market conditions are always susceptible to rapid change, as we have seen before, and at the time of this writing the markets are again good. Worst-case scenario, at least we will know how to better play the great game of business and have a few, perhaps premature, gray hairs of experience.

The 15-Phase Process of Closing a Round

The process of raising venture funding generally goes something like this. Depending on the stage you've reached, your experience and reputation, and connections, some of these phases can be skipped.

1. *The introduction:* You get introduced to a firm through a entrepreneur the firm has previously invested in, an investor they've worked with in the past, or a trusted attorney they know.
2. *The initial review:* An associate at the firm reviews your executive summary and gives a cursory look at your full plan and projections, and if interested, schedules a call with you. It helps if you already have existing revenue or have had a previous successful venture.
3. *The first call:* You speak with the associate by phone about what you are doing.

4. *The partner discussion:* If the associate likes what you are doing, he or she speaks to a partner at the firm about the opportunity.

5. *The first meeting:* If you can get the interest of a partner, he or she will invite you to the firm's offices to meet you, or meet at your office if you have an office, depending on the partner's level of interest and your location. During this first meeting you will generally discuss your:

   a. Background and experience
   b. Team makeup
   c. Competition
   d. Product differentiation
   e. Market size
   f. Funding needs

6. *The valuation discussion:* After the first meeting, if the partner remains interested, he or she may attempt to feel you out for the target valuation you are seeking. The partner also may choose not to discuss valuation and simply make an offer with the term sheet. If you are in a position of strength, you may wish to discuss valuation up front yourself so you don't waste time. Be prepared with comparable revenue multiples both from public companies and from private comparables that are similar to yours. These are called *comps.* Depending on many factors (team, technology, industry stage, revenue growth, market size), you can expect to be able to raise funds at 2× to 10× your revenues from the trailing 12 months or 1× to 4× your projected revenues from the next 12 months. If you don't have any revenues yet, the valuation will be whatever you can negotiate with an investor, based in part upon your experience and any intellectual property you have. At the end of the day, the market valuation for your company is what an investor is willing to pay—and as such, it is important to have multiple firms competing to invest in your company if possible. Depending on the stage of your company, you might be able

to raise funds at a 30 percent to 60 percent discount off the public market trailing or forward revenue comparables.

7. *The partner presentation:* If you can come to a general valuation range that both of you are comfortable with, the partner may invite you to present in person or via videoconference to the firm's full partner team. Prepare well and give a knockout presentation. Invest in a graphic designer to make your presentation look nice; go heavy on actual examples of customer use and light on complex slides. Don't let any slide have more than five bullet points or 50 words. Your presentation is likely to be between 15 and 60 minutes. Ask in advance how long the firm would like you to present for.

8. *The initial due diligence:* After the presentation to the full partner team, if the partners like the deal, they may ask for some additional due diligence items, such as your full financials, and want to speak with other members of your team and some of your customers.

9. *The term sheet:* If all goes well during the initial due diligence phase, the venture firm will likely provide you with a term sheet. A term sheet is generally around two to eight pages long and is an indication of interest in investing in you. With a term sheet, the investment firm attempts to create agreement around the general terms of the deal before the lawyers create the more extensive 20- to 40-page investment agreement document. Depending on the amount of money you are raising, sometimes you will raise money from multiple firms at once in a syndicate deal. If this is the case, one firm will likely lead the deal and the other firm(s) will agree to the same term sheet. Often the first interested firm will be able to bring syndicate partners to the table, although sometimes you may need to find them yourself.

10. *The attorney review:* Once you receive a term sheet, have your attorney review it right away and provide feedback before you discuss it with the investment firm. Your company will likely have to pay the attorney fees for your lawyer and the lawyers from the firm. You can expect to pay

between $15,000 and $40,000 to each firm, depending on the amount of money you are raising and the complexity of the deal. Make sure you cap in the term sheet the amount of legal fees your firm will pay upon close.

11. *The term sheet negotiation:* Once you have reviewed the term sheet with your attorney, have a follow-up conversation with the partner or associate you are dealing with to negotiate it. Make sure you know which terms are the most important to you going into any negotiation (generally the valuation, option pool size, liquidation preference, participating preferred, founder revesting, and preferred stock veto rights). You may wish to have your attorney (or CFO if you have one) negotiate the finer points directly with the firm's attorney. At this point it is critical to have a top-tier venture attorney on your side. These attorneys generally bill between $250 and $500 per hour, depending on their experience and the market. Your negotiating power will be based upon:

a. How much you need the money
b. The reputation of the firm
c. Your reputation as an entrepreneur
d. Any past successes you've had
e. Your experience
f. The quality of your management team
g. The members of your advisory panel
h. The size of your addressable market
i. Your market timing
j. The quality of your technology and IP
k. Your ability to walk away
l. Whether you have other competing term sheets

Know that it is generally taboo to provide specifics to one firm about another firm's term sheet, but you can often provide generalities or refer to wanting to have a competitive process in order to have more power in negotiating the term sheet. Do not sign the term sheet until you have negotiated it to your satisfaction and your attorney approves signing it.

Once you sign a term sheet, it is very difficult to negotiate any changes in the final document. If you can create a parallel process and receive multiple term sheets, you will have more power. It often will take three or four negotiation iterations to get a term sheet both sides are happy with. It can take a lot of time (and a few thousand dollars of attorney fees) to effectively accomplish this—and might be impossible without the right experience and revenues. We were unable to create a truly competitive process during our seed round, but we did accomplish a competitive round in our Series A after we had $6 million in annual revenues, great technology, and rapid growth. While it can take six to eight weeks after the first meeting to get a term sheet from a venture firm traditionally, once you have an existing term sheet you may be able to get competing term sheets in as little as one to two weeks. Group mentality does at times take hold, causing the valuation to be bid up with multiple players in the deal and some of the secondary terms to be softened. This noted, at some point it can be unhealthy to push the valuation up. The highest bidders are not always the best firm for you to work with.

12. *The term sheet signing:* Agree to the general terms of the deal and either digitally sign the term sheet or sign in person.

13. *The full due diligence:* Once you sign the term sheet, a more extensive due diligence list will be provided to you. This list may include items such as:

   a. Detailed sales pipeline
   b. Revenue by customer type
   c. Detailed operational plan and budget
   d. Full business plan
   e. Hiring plan
   f. Detailed revenue assumptions
   g. Audited financial statements
   h. Bank reconciliation detail
   i. Product pricing list
   j. Detailed product road map

k. Customer, employee, insurance, and lease contracts

l. Relevant white papers and analyst coverage

m. Details on IT infrastructure

n. Current partner list

o. Lead generation processes

p. Customer satisfaction survey

q. Customer reference list

r. Details on intellectual property

s. Current capitalization chart with options detail

t. Organizational chart

u. Salary and bonus structure for company

v. Employee turnover

w. Management background checks

x. Competitive analysis

y. Expected acquirers

z. Past board meeting minutes

14. *The final investment documents:* Once this due diligence is complete, if all goes well, you will receive the final investment documents from the investment firm's lawyers. Have your attorney review it closely and negotiate any needed changes. Pay especially close attention to any representations and warranties you are making as an officer of the company and personally. The final investment documents generally include a:

   a. Share purchase agreement

   b. Investor rights agreement

   c. Right of first refusal and cosale agreement

   d. Voting agreement

15. *The deal signing:* Provide your company bank account information, close the deal, watch the funds go into your account, breathe a sigh of relief, send out the press release, and welcome your new investor(s) and board member(s) to the team with a celebration open house, exchange of company swag, and thank-you card. Then get going on growing revenue.

The Key Terms of a Venture Term Sheet

The Offering Terms

- *Closing dates:* The target date for the close of the deal.
- *Investors:* Which firm(s) will invest in the deal.
- *Amount raised:* How much money you are investing.
- *Premoney valuation:* The agreed-upon value of your company before the investment.
- *Postmoney valuation:* The value of your company after the investment. Equal to the premoney valuation plus the investment amount.
- *Capitalization:* The company's current shareholder list with the number of shares and options each shareholder has.
- *Use of proceeds:* How the investment money is to be used.

The Charter

- *Dividends:* The process by which dividends will be distributed to shareholders. Dividend distribution generally occurs at the discretion of the board. This section also includes the interest rate at which the investment funds will grow each year, on either a cumulative or a noncumulative basis. Try to negotiate out any interest or at least request no interest in the case of a successful exit.
- *Liquidation preference:* The right for the investors to receive their money out first in a liquidity event before payment is made to common shareholders.
- *Voting rights:* Covers the rights of the investor(s) to vote on certain items materially affecting the company.
- *Protective provisions:* Describes what company changes need to be approved by the investor(s).
- *Antidilution provisions:* The right of the investors to be protected from dilution in the event that stock is ever sold at a price less than the current round (called a down-round). The broad-based weighted average is the method of calculating dilution that is most company-friendly.

- *Mandatory conversion:* Describes the conditions and process by which the preferred shares convert into common shares.
- *Optional conversion:* The right for the investors to convert their preferred shares into common shares at any point in time.
- *Redemption rights:* The right of the investors to get their money back if they choose after a period of time, generally after five years. This is a rarely used provision, but be careful with it nonetheless.

Stock Purchase Agreement
- *Representations and warranties:* The representations the company must make to be true and accurate for the investment to take place.
- *Conditions to closing:* A general description of the due diligence area to be looked at prior to closing.
- *Counsel and expenses:* Covers the maximum amount of money due to the attorneys to close the deal. This amount is generally between $10,000 and $30,000, depending on the complexity of the deal. The company generally will pay this out of the investment amount.

Investor Rights Agreement
- *Registration rights:* Refers to the rights of the investors to register their shares during a public offering.
- *Information and inspection rights:* The rights of the investor to receive information about the company.
- *Board matters:* The composition of the board of directors following the deal. Do your best to ensure that there are more company representatives than investor representatives. You effectively lose control of the company if this is not the case. You may wish your board to consist of your CEO, chairman, or CFO, and one investor, or expand the size to five members and have your CEO, CFO, chairman, and two investor representatives.

(Continued)

- *Drag along:* The right of the board and preferred shareholders to ensure that all stockholders will agree to a sign if the board and majority of the preferred stockholders agree to sell.
- *Right of first refusal:* The right of the company and/or the investors to purchase any shares that any shareholder chooses to sell.

Other Matters

- *Bank debt:* Any related line of credit that the investors expressly approve.
- *Employment matters:* A condition of closing requiring all employees to have employment contracts and noncompete agreements.
- *No shop/confidentiality:* An agreement not to tell anyone outside of company shareholders, the board of directors, and your attorney about the terms of the deal or to seek other term sheets during a period of usually 30 to 45 days while the deal is being closed.
- *Binding/nonbinding provisions:* Any obligations to which the term sheet will legally bind the parties, whether or not the deal is executed, such as paying the legal fees of the investors.
- *Expiration:* The date after which the term sheet offer is no longer valid. Don't let this date force you into signing the term sheet before you are ready. It is usually made up.

As you can see, the process can be arduous and long, especially if you are dealing with multiple firms and trying to parallel process to create a competitive round. At the end of the day, even if a firm is not interested, try to build a relationship for the future.

It takes time to learn about the many components of a term sheet. It can be worthwhile to have an attorney or CFO who can guide you through the process. At the end of the day, don't sign the term sheet until you are fully comfortable with it and understand the provisions within.

Bootstrapping

It is certainly possible to create a successful company without any initial investment other than time and energy. This is often the only option available to young entrepreneurs. Here's what you can expect if you go this route.

1. Be prepared (and able) to work 70+-hour weeks for a year or more without any salary.
2. Be prepared to wear multiple hats including those of CEO, CFO, COO, VP of marketing, VP of business development, and chief executive janitor.
3. Be prepared to offer ownership in your company to other team members until you can pay them a market salary.
4. Be open to looking at creative ways of getting legal and accounting advisors to provide discounted help, including offering them a small piece of the pie.

CEO and Chief Executive Janitor

When a company is started, unless there is ample financing, the owner will often find himself or herself all alone for a while until sales start picking up and cash flow can support hiring help. My friend and business partner Aaron Houghton once told me, "As a start-up CEO you are the chief executive officer, chief executive painter, and chief executive janitor." Now, clearly this is not the case if you are backed by venture capital or have enough funds to bankroll a staff. However, many people simply do not have much capital they can invest, do not have access to venture capitalists, or simply wish to avoid going into debt or selling off part of their company. Office space for these people, at least at first, often consists of dorm rooms, garages, or third bedrooms.

(Continued)

So how do you get past this start-up phase? What are some ways to start building cash flow? And at what point do you invest in things like office space, intellectual property protection, accounting software, inventory, or employees?

As I related in Chapter 1, in August 2001 I met a man who had founded a number of companies and was working on his next. When I came on board, everything had been put in place and the groundwork had been done. The business owner had developed the product and had spent the past year laying the foundation for the company that would sell that product. Only a few hundred dollars in sales had been made to that point, but things were ready to take off.

A year later, the company was nearing $200,000 in sales each month and was close to passing the $1 million mark in sales. This company, however, never raised a dime of venture capital and never even took on any debt. This was a bootstrapped company from start to finish. In June 2002, I had a chance to interview the owner of that company. Here's what he said on the topic of bootstrapping his company.

First of all, if you are on a tight budget, be ever mindful that the last thing you need is overhead. Don't put the cart before the horse. Find a product. There are products out there. Look through the classifieds. There are people out there who have wonderful products but do not know how to market them. Contact these individuals and make them an offer. Give them a small piece of the action and buy out the product from them or license it. If you do not have money, find investors. Just make sure you retain control of the company. There are books available that can show you how to draft sample agreements like this.

The small entrepreneur simply needs to learn that much can happen in his or her own garage. You can take a product, spend a minimal amount of money to get a label on it and packaging, and take it out door-to-door to small shops. Go to these shops and tell them you'd like to put the product in on a consignment basis. You may run into trouble with stores asking for credit, but do what you can and extend credit if you are able to get some initial cash flow.

Then take your product and sell it to your friends. If your product is as good as you say it is, those same friends are going to be telling their friends. You can expand from a simple little platform like this.

Then build your Web site, get an affiliate program started, and go from there. The key is finding a superior product that can be manufactured at a very low cost. The typical successful television product needs a 7× markup (600 percent). Educate yourself about markups and costs.

Packaging is essential. Spend more on your packaging and written materials. If you cannot write, find a copywriter who can. Get out and talk to people, and get feedback on your product as often as you can.

If you have a superior product, you'll win the battle. If you do not, odds are, you are going to lose.

Learn to do what you can yourself. Don't walk into a lawyer's office and spend $2,500 needlessly. Find an incorporation mill that can do it for $250. Learn how to write copy—that's really essential.

If you make a mistake, be sure you learn from that mistake. If you fail, be sure you learn from the failure. I've not known a successful entrepreneur who didn't have four or five failures. I might be a notable exception. I've failed only two or three times [laugh].

Just keep punching. It's tenacity that wins.

Very powerful words from a man who built a very successful company. If you find yourself in a position without too much money, but you do not want to take on debt or sell off stock, internalize these words.

(*Continued*)

Doing the groundwork for a new company can take time. Common jobs include sourcing products; filing articles of incorporation; printing letterhead, business cards, and brochures; writing sales copy; finding office space; developing a Web site; negotiating contracts with suppliers; purchasing an initial inventory; registering a trademark; and buying office supplies.

In August 2001, when I began working with the nutraceuticals company, there was not enough cash flow to hire any employees yet, so the owner and I had to do everything. The axiom about being both CEO and janitor rang true indeed for the owner, while I was a jack-of-all-trades myself. I handled all the e-mails, the phones, the packaging of orders, the marketing, the walk-in customers, the affiliates, and the Web site. The owner handled the bankers, the forms, the accounting, and the most important customers. By no means were we in Silicon Valley in 1999 and by no means did the company have millions of dollars of venture capital.

After incorporating, the company went 5 months before obtaining office space and 11 months before getting any outside help. After bringing me on as an independent contractor, no one else was hired for three additional months.

Soon, however, we began to have enough orders for the product to require a part-time person to package the orders and take them to the post office. This position soon became full-time as more and more orders came in. This person also kept track of the inventory of all supplies and reordered items as needed.

By February, the company had grown to the point where I was spending much of my time answering the phones and e-mails instead of marketing. At this point, the company hired someone to take care of customer service. This person took over all the customer service e-mails and answered the phones, allowing me to concentrate on growing sales. In April, the company hired an eventual replacement for me—someone whom I could train in my marketing methodology and practices before I left for college that August.

Finally, in July, the company brought on an accountant to take over as chief financial officer. The company had been having trouble with the merchant account processor, and the expenses were starting to grow. The CFO handled payroll, took checks to the bank, and went over the expense reports and merchant account figures with a fine-tooth comb.

Start with a good product, do the groundwork and due diligence well, don't skimp when acquiring good advisors, put the proper marketing systems into place, get the right people on your team, then mix in a little time and an ounce of perseverance. Finally, just remember as you toil away endless days and endless nights on your dream, on your baby, on your future million-dollar company, that the entrepreneurial gods are with you and cheering you on, every step of the way.

8

STEP 6: DEVELOP YOUR PRODUCT

★

Never before in history has innovation offered promise of so much to so many in so short a time.

—BILL GATES

If you want to make a lot of money in business, in general, you have to do one of two things. You have to either create a new product or create a new business model—or invest in a business that is doing this. You have to innovate or be an innovation enabler.

Michael Dell created a new business model with his direct-to-consumer distribution of personal computers. So did Henry Ford with his mass-production assembly line, John D. Rockefeller with his vertically integrated oil empire, Ray Kroc with McDonald's, and Pierre Omidyar with eBay. Others, however, from Thomas Edison to Wally Amos, have made their money from product innovation. In this chapter, we'll talk about the stages involved in developing a product.

> "If you want to make a lot of money you have to do one of two things. You have to either create a new product or create a new business model."

The Perfect Product

While most established businesses have more than one stream of revenue, it is often the sale of products that contributes most to cash flow. The products a company sells will be a huge factor in whether the company succeeds. The right product can propel any company to fortune, and the wrong product can make even the most exhaustive efforts unprofitable.

So what are the attributes of good products? As we learned from examining the MAR Model of Opportunity Evaluation, one of the most important requirements of a product is that it fulfill a need or want. Does the product ease a pain, fulfill a dream, make life easier, or make life better? If not, you better start searching for a product that does. The first part of the executive summary in any business plan addresses the need. What is the need, and how does your business/product fulfill this need?

The second part of the executive summary is an overview of the market. What is the market for the product? Is it a business-to-business product or business-to-consumer? How big is the market? In some cases, having a product with mass-market appeal is a good thing. For example, if you wanted to have your product featured on the Home Shopping Network or market it using infomercials, then you want your potential customers to be everyone or at least a large part of the population. Products with a mass-market appeal that have been successfully marketed through infomercials include George Foreman Grills, Ginsu knives, and OxiClean cleaner. On the other hand, it is unlikely that you would be successful marketing a book analyzing the cerebral cortexes of llamas via a mass-market infomercial.

Other times, however, it is beneficial to have a product that is geared to a niche market. It is much easier to become a real player with niche products than with products that appeal to everyone. There is generally less competition, plus you are able to focus your marketing and advertising on a predetermined demographic group. In most cases, there will already be trade journals, Web sites, and magazines to which the market segment you are targeting pays attention, making it much easier to develop brand recognition and a product following. Word of mouth, also known as *viral marketing,* tends to spread faster with these niche products, and it is quite likely that someone with a specific need knows a few other people with the same need.

The Importance of an Ample Margin

Sufficient markup is a crucial attribute of a good product. Generally, the markup ratio must be at least 2:1. However, the best products have markups of 5:1 or more. This translates to a 400 percent or more markup. You might say, "If I raised my prices that high, no one would ever buy." This might be true, depending on your product and the competition in your industry. However, there are a number of things you can do to increase your markup, and, hence, your per-product profit margin, without reducing the number of sales.

First, let's define *markup*. Markup is simply the sale price of the product divided by the cost of the goods sold. This equation has two components and can be worked on from two angles. The first angle is to lower your cost of goods sold. How? Do everything you can to get the lowest possible price from your supplier(s). Renegotiate terms, offer incentives, tell them you'll be sending some business their way—whatever you need to do to get their lowest price. Second, increase your sale price. How can this be done without hurting sales? Simple: increase the perceived value of your product.

Perceived value is what customers think your product should cost or, more specifically, the value they think it has to them and what they would be willing to pay for it.

Improving Perceived Value

Here are eight ways to improve the perceived value of your product:

1. Emphasize quality.
2. Display success stories on your Web site and in your marketing materials.
3. Promote your top-quality customer service.
4. Stress convenience.
5. Improve the design of your product's packaging and labeling.

6. Distinguish your product from your competitors' products and explain why yours is best.
7. Develop your unique selling proposition.
8. If you are selling this product from your Web site, make sure the site is nicely designed, easy to use, and typo free.

After you've improved the perceived value of your product, you should be able to increase its price without causing a decrease in net profits.

One-Time Sale or Continued Sales?

J. Paul Getty, a former billionaire oil baron and once the richest man in the world, is known for emphasizing the importance of selling products that yield continued sales. Most products are single-sale items (vacuums, beds, ladders, videos, etc.); it is more difficult to build a business selling these because you are always spending money and time trying to attract new customers. If you have your choice of products, look for those that can be sold multiple times to the same customer.

The pharmaceutical industry can afford to spend the billions it does on research and development. Why? Simply because most often they produce treatments, not cures, for diseases and ailments. Treatments must be taken continuously. Other health products like nutraceuticals and vitamins are also repeat-sale products. Anything that needs to be refilled or reordered within a relatively short time frame can be considered a repeat-sale product. The majority of services (phone, water, electricity, hosting, etc) are on this autobill and autodeliver system. See if you can find a way to put your product on an autobill and autoship system. And if you can't, find a product or service to sell that you can.

Up-Sell and Cross-Sell Ability

A good marketer knows the value of up-selling and cross-selling. In a business, there are three ways to increase revenue: (1) increase the number of customers you have, (2) increase the frequency at which your customers buy from you, and (3) increase the amount they spend on each purchase. Up-selling and cross-selling work on this third strategy. Essentially, up-selling is encouraging (usually through an incentive such as a discount or free gift) customers at the time of sale to purchase more of your product than they had originally intended. Cross-selling is selling the same customers a product related to the one they are buying that they either were not intending to buy in the first place or didn't know you offered.

Here's an example of an up-sell and a cross-sell. One year when I was in high school, I wanted to buy a small turtle for my girlfriend, Kristina, for Christmas. So I drove to the pet store and walked in with the intention of buying a turtle, some turtle food, and a fish bowl to put the turtle in. Well, $87 later I walked out with a lovely new turtle, a glass aquarium, an automatic filter, an aquarium heater, two bags of stones, turtle pellets, and some dead crickets. Walking out, I realized that I had been both up-sold and cross-sold by an experienced salesperson.

Similar to the concepts of up-selling and cross-selling is the back-end product. The back-end product is a related and often more expensive product offered to customers after they've purchased their first product. Using back-ends, cross-selling, and up-selling is a great way to strengthen your bottom line. Therefore, before deciding to sell a product, it is necessary to determine how easily a product can be up-sold and cross-sold and whether there are any suitably related products to offer your customers after they've made an initial purchase.

The Perfect Product in Review

The perfect product has the following attributes:

1. It fulfills a need or want.
2. It has either niche market appeal or mass-market appeal.
3. It has at least a 2:1 markup ratio; 5:1 or higher is optimal.
4. It has a high perceived value.
5. It must be replenished or repurchased by the customer often.

6. It is easily up-sold and cross-sold.
7. It has a related back-end product.

On August 1, 2001, I first met the owner of the health products company that I worked for during my senior year of high school. He had found a great product and had worked the past year laying the groundwork to create the company that would sell that product. I wasn't sure at the time just how good his product was. A year later, however, as we neared the $1 million mark in sales, I knew.

The market size was huge. The demand for the product was large and increasing. The product was of high quality. The product was unique and could be distinguished easily from competing products. The product was effective. The product offered significant benefits to the consumer. The product had to be reordered every 30 days. The product could be obtained at a relatively low cost, which supported a large markup. Finally, there were few serious competitors selling similar products.

In short, it was a great product. But how do you know if your product is great? And if you are in search of a product to sell, what questions must you ask to determine that it is great and will sell well?

There are two factors that must be assessed when selecting a product: the inherent qualities of the product and the state of the marketplace. Here is a list of questions to ask when examining each of your products or potential products.

How to Tell If Your Product Is Great: The Inherent Qualities of the Product

1. Is the product of high quality?
2. Is the product effective?
3. How valuable are the benefits the product gives to the consumer?
4. Does the product increase pleasure, increase utility, or reduce pain?
5. Must the product be reordered?
6. Can a back-end product be developed easily?

How to Tell If Your Product Is Great: The State of the Marketplace

1. Can it be obtained or produced for a low cost so as to support a high margin?
2. What is the current demand for the product?
3. Is this demand expanding?
4. How many other competitors are selling the same or a similar product?
5. How many serious competitors are there?
6. What are the sales figures of these competitors?
7. What are the product's substitutes?
8. Are there any factors that might increase or decrease sales of substitutes?
9. How hard will it be to differentiate the product from competing products?

Creating Your Product

The first phase in creating a product is to determine whether you will be manufacturing it in-house or outsourcing the manufacturing. In cases where production requires heavy and expensive machinery, you should outsource production initially. In cases where the needed equipment can be purchased fairly inexpensively, it may be more cost effective to purchase the equipment yourself.

If you choose to produce your product(s) yourself, you'll need to source (find suppliers for) all the parts and machinery required. If you will be outsourcing everything to a manufacturing partner, you'll need to submit a request for quote (RFQ) from potential manufacturers. You'll describe exactly what you need done and then evaluate the possibilities based on the information and price quotes you receive in return. Here are two stories about young entrepreneurs I've met who have developed products.

When I first met my friend Erik Severinghaus, he was developing a product that would allow, at the touch of a button, information to be passed from a small hub to a PDA device. Erik envisioned that the device could be used at trade shows to quickly transfer information from a company to a prospect or from a prospect to a company, between businesspersons, or at the front desks of hotels. He had incorporated a company, FastCAT, Inc., to sell the product and had spent over a year developing it.

Erik used the skills he had learned as a network and systems engineer to modify a computer chip process to load and wirelessly transfer the needed information. He then constructed a half-sphere case out of a light cover and a piece of PVC pipe. He sourced a press button and connected the button to the chip. He learned about the transfer standards with the major PDA operating systems, and finally, after more than a year of work, got the device to function.

His next action was to raise the funding he needed so he could hire a graphic designer to redesign the casing to make it look less like a science project and more like a high-technology device, locate a manufacturer, and outsource the production of a functioning prototype with the new design. Unfortunately, Erik was unable to find the funding, and he soon moved on to other ventures. His story provides a good illustration of just how many stages there are in developing a product.

In February 2003, I met Dan Bowman and Chirag Nanavati. Dan and Chirag had been developing a technology that provided a more efficient, healthy, and tasty way to remove fat from potato chips. While Dan was a first-year MBA student at UNC Kenan Flagler Business School, he was working for the Office of Technology Development and was looking through UNC's intellectual property portfolio. He found out that professors at UNC and North Carolina State University had developed a method of using carbon dioxide to extract the fat from snack foods. Dan talked to the Technology Transfer Office and obtained permission to build a company to commercialize this technology.

The first thing to do was choose the application. After completing market research, Dan decided that he would start up by building a machine that would take the fat out of potato chips. He went through the process of finding a manufacturer that could produce such equipment and worked with them over many months to develop a working prototype. During that time, he brought on as partners Chirag and Randy Diefenthal and came up with the company name of Singras. Finally, just in time to present at the Venture Capital Investment Competition in February 2003, the manufacturing firm devised a prototype machine to produce the chips. They were excited to bring their first batch to the competition.

These brief stories only begin to illustrate the number of stages and the difficulty of creating certain types of products. The process of naming a product, obtaining a trademark, designing labels and packaging, evaluating manufacturers, and navigating the patent application can be complex. If you have the right team, good technology, and a reliable partner in your supplier, you can do it. The benefits are often worth it.

You might be developing a product that is not so difficult to produce. Perhaps you are starting a T-shirt printing company or writing an e-book you will sell online. Or perhaps you are not selling a product at all. This is fine as well. Just make sure that if you are developing a product, you keep in mind the aforementioned key points regarding creating a good product.

The Product Management Process

One of the biggest perils of being a new company as it grows from a fledgling organization into a multi-million-dollar corporation and eventually into great worldwide company is developing a product or service over multiple product cycles from the first iteration to subsequent variations. Whether the product is software and you're working with versions or it's a consumer goods product and you're improving a feature or changing the design or functionality, getting the ongoing process of product development right is key to a company's success. There's a process of innovation you must go through, and you can do it either correctly or incorrectly.

Your ability to put in place the right product innovation and R&D processes within your organization makes a big impact on your long-term success. It is possible to build the first version of a product and make a few hundred thousand dollars in sales, then not continue to innovate. Within a year to 18 months, however, a new product cycle will come along in the market. Regardless of the business you are in, if you're not reinvesting part of the money you're making into improving your service, improving your product, and listening to your customers so that you know how to improve your product and service, you are going to fall behind in a fairly short time.

> "The first principle of creating a great product management process is to listen to your customers."

The first principle of creating a great product management process is to listen to your customers. Survey them. Ask them what they like, how you can improve the features the product already offers, and what features and services you can provide in addition to the existing ones. Asking these questions is critical.

We hired iContact's chief technical officer in February 2004, bringing him on as a lead developer. He was our fourth employee. He started out writing codes and within a month we had a new surveying product, and within another month we had a new autoresponder feature. The process was fairly quick, since we had only one programmer. Over the past four years iContact's technical department has evolved from having a single developer to having a team of 16 full-time developers, a user interface engineer, a database administrator, a quality assurance team, and a systems administration team.

Now, out of necessity, we go through a formal iteration process. We have a formal product wish list, a tracking tool called Xplanner to monitor our progress, a bug tracking tool called Bugzilla, and product stories submitted by employees and refined by directors.

We have a monthly sprint review process in which we review all the work we've done over the past four weeks. We have a sprint planning meeting where we plan for the next four weeks and decide what we're going to develop. We have a product management meeting every two weeks. We are constantly seeking input. We seek data through customer surveys, customer focus groups, feedback forms on the Web site and application, and competing products. This ensures that we are aware of the customer-requested features as well as the features we need to create to lead the market with the current version of our product.

Product management at iContact is a more agile process now. We use sticky notes, note cards, voting systems, surveying tools, and various meetings and procedures. This flexible innovation process has been critical to iContact's success. We used to have a six-month development cycle during which we would create a products requirements document consisting of 30 or 40 pages saying this is what we want; then we'd give it to the developers, and they'd have six months to develop that product. When we released, we found that the necessary quality assurance level wasn't there. We were losing so much dynamism by having such a long process. In response, iContact switched to a four-week sprint and a scrum style of development that has been beneficial.

Regardless of the type of company that you are building, think critically about how your product innovation process and your product management process can work together to create a system of constant improvements. Consistent improvement is what capitalism and the competitive market economy are all about, and what the real role of an entrepreneur is.

> "Consistent improvement is what capitalism and the competitive market economy are all about, and what the real role of an entrepreneur is."

The Japanese have a theory called *kaizen,* which means "continuous improvement." If you can take something you have today and, as money comes in, reinvest that money to make it better and better, you will be able to provide a better-quality service or product at a lower cost. This constant improvement enables you to expand the scale of your marketplace and create a lasting and very large organization that is profitable for yourself and your shareholders, as well as for the customers using your products.

9

STEP 7: DEVELOP YOUR MARKETING AND SALES STRATEGY

Two shoe salesmen find themselves in a rustic backward part of Africa. The first salesman wires back to his head office: "There is no prospect of sales. Natives do not wear shoes!" The other salesman wires: "No one wears shoes here. We can dominate the market. Send all possible stock."

—Akio Morita, Sony

What Is Marketing?

Marketing is everything you do to place your product or service in the hands of potential customers. The purpose of marketing is to get the word out about your product—and in turn to make sales of your product or service. While sales is the act of converting a prospect into a customer, marketing is the process that generates prospects and makes sales possible, including brand development, partnership creation, publicity, and advertising.

Marketing is the background work that gets prospects in the door. Sales is the process of converting those prospects to lifetime customers. The reason many businesses fail is a breakdown in, or lack of, marketing. You can develop a wonderful product or provide a high-value-add service, but if no one knows about it, your business will not succeed.

Although marketing can be complex, the basics of marketing are simple! Here are the key questions to ask as you develop your marketing plan:

1. Who is likely to buy my product or service?
2. Where do these people look for products or services like mine?
3. How can I get into those places?

There are two different types of marketing. The type you'll learn in most business schools can be generally defined as corporate or brand marketing. In a business school class on corporate marketing, you'll learn about things like branding strategy, demographics, and positioning statements. While these subjects are important to know, they will not be of great benefit to the bootstrapping entrepreneur who does not have a million-dollar budget, 10 ad designers, and a sales force of 100. The other type of marketing is entrepreneurial marketing. In entrepreneurial marketing, instead of concentrating on brand recognition, you concentrate on sales and lead generation. Without much money to spend, the return on investment (ROI) of every ad, every campaign, is that much more important.

This chapter presents the basics of marketing, the core of much of what corporate marketing is based on as well as a complete step-by-step entrepreneurial marketing strategy for launching your business and building it to $1 million in sales at a low cost.

The Four Ps

One of the most basic and most important concepts in marketing is known as the Four Ps: product, price, place, and promotion. If you

Important Definitions for Marketers

B2B: Business to business.

B2C: Business to consumer.

Brand: The aggregate representation and reputation of your business across all those who interact with it. Includes much more than simply the logo and corporate identity.

CAC: Customer acquisition cost.

CRM: Customer relationship management.

CTR: Click-through rate.

Demographics: Data on customers and prospects such as gender, location, birth date, past purchases, income level, and marital status. Marketers can better target their promotions with good demographic data.

Direct-to-consumer: Selling products directly to buyers without any intermediaries.

Distribution model: The levels of companies through which a product is sourced, manufactured, and then sold.

Distribution strategy: Where and how a company positions itself in the value chain, including what type of distribution model it follows.

LTV: The lifetime value (of a customer).

Market research: Research about a market including the competitors and competing products, its size, and growth rate.

Retail: Selling a product to an end buyer.

ROAS: Return on ad spend.

ROI: Return on investment.

Target market: Those whom your business will be targeting with the promotions for your product. Those who are most likely to buy.

USP: Unique selling point, also known as the value proposition; what you do that differentiates you from your competitors.

Value chain: A representation of the distribution model based on the value added by each type of business at each level.

Wholesale: Selling of a product to another business that will later resell it.

can develop a good product at the right price, position it in a place where buyers are, and promote it well to create desire in the customers' mind, you'll quickly succeed in making a lot of sales.

Product

As previously discussed, your product is crucial to your success. If you have a good product, getting the other three Ps right will be that much easier. *Product* includes both the actual physical product and product decisions such as function, appearance, packaging, labeling, and warranty. The word *product* also encompasses any services you may provide.

Price

If your price is too high, not enough people will be able to afford it. If your price is too low, you will not make any profit. Furthermore, if your price is too low, many will not buy the product because they see it as an inferior good. To best manage these variables and optimize your net profits, you will have to test various prices for your product(s).

Place

Place is essential to building sales. Place rests on *positioning*—the positioning of your marketing message and the positioning of your product. In retail stores, the corporate market, and online, properly positioning your product is a very important skill. Without proper positioning, no one will know you exist. If you are hidden in the back corner of a store on the bottom shelf and your Web site is number 3,425 in the search engines for your targeted keywords, you likely will not make many sales, no matter how good the product is. We'll talk more about how to position your product both online and off later in this chapter.

The positioning of your product is also known as your *distribution strategy*. A distribution strategy is developed by determining where on the *value chain* you want your business to be positioned and who the buyer will be. You may sell your product to a retail store, which then resells it to a buyer, a manufacturer who sells exclusively to jobbers and regional representatives, or directly to end consumers. We'll talk more about distribution models and strategies later in this chapter.

Promotion

Promotion is an essential part of the marketing process. Promotion decisions include those related to communicating your message, advertising, and public relations.

Market Research and Competitive Intelligence

As noted earlier, when you write your business plan, you will need to complete research on the state of the marketplace. Five good sources for quality market information are Hoover's Online, Lexis-Nexis, Factiva, ZoomInfo, and Dialog. These are all paid services, but they can be worth the investment if you can properly leverage the information in their extensive databases. And if, by chance, you are a university student, contact your librarian, as you might have free access to these services. If you are not a student, make a visit to your local library. Many libraries have either subscriptions to these services or static versions of the databases on CD.

To complete your market research, it is always a good idea to talk to potential customers. You can create a survey and send it out to potential customers using a tool such as iContact, or hold a focus group with a related organization in your area. If you have a prototype of a product you are working on, you can ask potential customers about everything from design to functionality. Because you are an aspiring entrepreneur, many people will be willing to help you. Be sure to take advantage of this.

Generally, your research will help you uncover several target markets that you can reach with your product or service. It is important to, as specifically as you can, describe each of your target markets. You may define one of your target markets as married males, ages 30 to 45, living in Hoboken, New Jersey, or all persons over the age of 60 who suffer from type 2 diabetes. You can surely have more than one target market; these are known as *market segments*. For example, your product might be effective for both senior citizens and athletes. Surely, you'll want to have different marketing materials for each segment.

If you can, attempt to determine who your customers are, how many there are, where they are, what needs they have that are not currently being met, why they buy, and from whom they buy.

At iContact, we have created five personas that represent each of our distinct markets:

1. Carl: The contract Web designer living in a big city.
2. Karen: The work-at-home mom who scrapbooks in her free time.
3. Frank: The president of a 10-person company.
4. Joe: The vice president of marketing at a 100-person company.
5. Eileen: The director of e-marketing at a Fortune 500 company.

Action Item 5: Create Your Target Personas

Create three to five personas for people who would be likely buyers of your product or service. What are their names? How old are they? Where do they live? What types of companies do they work for? What are their job titles? Where do they look for products like those you provide?

1. _____

2. _____

3. _____

4. _____

5. _____

Creating Your Distribution Strategy

Getting a product from parts to consumer in the old economy often involved five or more companies. There would be a parts supplier, a product manufacturer, a jobber, a wholesaler, and a retailer who would finally sell to the end consumer. With each intermediary there would have to be another markup. There was great inefficiency and prices were high.

Many companies today, however, are turning to a direct-to-consumer (DTC) model. Instead of five or six companies in the distribution chain, there are two: the supplier and the manufacturer. Now, because of the Internet and mail order, companies that once focused solely on creating can also build competencies in selling. All the manufacturer has to do is set up a Web site, get it to the top of the search engines, and hire a few people to ship out orders. And now, instead of a 40 percent markup, the manufacturer can charge a 400 percent markup—all because of the shift to a DTC strategy.

I learned this lesson very well working with a nutraceuticals company in 2001 and 2002. When I got there, the company was focusing on selling to local retailers. We soon shifted toward focusing on DTC Internet sales, taking the markup from 3× to 7×. Figure 9.1 is a chart that compares an old and a new distribution model.

As you can see from Figure 9.1, the new model is much more efficient. By selling directly to your customers instead of going through intermediaries whenever possible, you'll be able to increase your price while keeping your costs the same, greatly improving your gross and net margins.

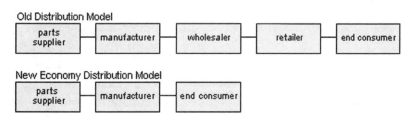

Figure 9.1 Old versus new distribution model.

In addition, by developing your consumer channel first, you'll create demand at the retail level. This is what happened with Icy Hot when marketing expert Jay Abraham got on board with the initial product developer to sell directly to consumers via mail order. Before they knew it, they had created a huge retail business in addition to their direct-to-consumer business. It's a lot easier to get into the GNCs, Wal-Marts, and Sears of the world when they have dozens of customers coming to them every day, asking why the store does not stock your product.

Although it may make sense in some cases to sell through traditional channels as a wholesaler, I'd encourage you to at least consider the possibility of selling your products directly to your customers, either via the Internet or via mail order. Of course, if your product is a high-ticket item or you are selling to businesses, you likely already have a sales force doing just this.

Building the Lifetime Value of a Customer

Many companies see the value of a customer as simply the value of all the purchases that customer has made to date. So if Sue has bought only one product worth $39, the company would see Sue as being worth $39 to them.

> The real and effectual discipline which is exercised over a workman is not that of his corporation, but that of his customer.
>
> **Adam Smith (1723–1790)**

Looking at the value of a customer in this manner is dangerous in that it really cannot give you any indication of the true lifetime value of your customers or the average expenditure of a customer with your company over the period of time between that customer's initial and final purchases. Assuming an average customer of yours purchases more than once from your company, this value will be higher than the value of the first sale. Your goal is to make this value as high as possible, of course.

Having a good idea of the true average lifetime value (LTV) of a customer is essential to knowing how much you are able to spend in acquiring each of your customers. For instance, if your average customer purchased a product worth $39 ten times from you, then their lifetime value would be $390. Knowing this information, you may, in fact, be able to spend more than $39 in acquiring each customer and still make a profit in the long run, depending on your cost of goods sold and operating expenses.

Another great reason to determine the lifetime value of an average customer for your company is so you can have a quantifiable goal. Once you have a quantified figure, you can create goals such as "In quarter three I want to increase my average LTV by 10 percent." These types of specific goals have a much greater chance of being accomplished than if you were to say, "I want to increase the lifetime value of my customers."

Essentially, increasing the lifetime value of your customers comes down to three objectives: increasing the length of time customers buy from you, increasing the amount they spend on each purchase, and decreasing the time between purchases. The following sections discuss three objectives designed to increase the lifetime value of your customers.

Objective 1: Personalize the Relationship and Build Rapport

Building rapport with customers is very important. Too many businesses commoditize their product. You might have a product that you believe is the best in the world—and it may well be. But there are lots of other companies out there, and there are lots of other companies producing nearly the same product. You need to differentiate both your product and your company. You need to build a personal relationship between your customer and someone in the company—say, for example, the owner. You need to develop a relationship and build rapport and trust with the customer for both the company and that person. Personalize the interaction.

Instead of saying, let's do business with XYZ Corporation, the customer will think, "You know, I'm going to do business with Joe. I like Joe. Joe's been e-mailing me those great tips every month because I subscribe to his newsletter. I have a good relationship with Joe. He followed up with me and made sure I was doing okay. I talked to Joe on the phone last month; he gave me some great advice. I'm going to stay with Joe. Just because this other company's product is a few bucks cheaper, no matter, I know Joe, I trust Joe, and I am going to stay with Joe."

This customer is no longer saying, "I'm going to stay with XYZ Corporation." You have succeeded in decommoditizing your product and have taken a very positive step toward increasing the lifetime value of your customers.

Business is about building relationships, and you build these relationships through effective communication. You communicate with your suppliers, your employees, and your affiliates, but you also have to effectively communicate with your customers.

I've been saying "customers" to this point. But, in fact, you do not want customers. Let me say it again: You do not want customers. What you do want are clients. What you want is to turn your customers into clients. Because once they are your clients, they will value the relationship more and stay with your company a lot longer. The lifetime value of those people will be exponentially higher.

How do you turn customers into clients? Well, along with your product you must offer a service. You must offer the valuable service of your advice and care. You must be an expert on your product and the benefits your product offers, take those customers under your guiding wing, and offer them only your best advice. You must have a *strategy of preeminence* whereby you align your interests with your clients' interests and advise them in making the decisions that will best benefit them, no matter what the effects on short-term profits.

Instead of having a commoditized product that customers buy on the basis of price only, you need to have a differentiated product. Your customers need to have a personalized relationship with someone within your organization; and you need to turn these customers into clients by offering them quality advice.

Say you are selling a nutraceutical product that treats fibromyalgia. Instead of saying, "Buy my product because it is the best," say, "Buy this product because it will do this and this and this, and also be sure to exercise this joint and this joint, and you may wish to do this stretch, and, oh yes, I found this stretch to be good as well, and you might want to drink a bit more water, and be careful of these foods in your diet." Help your customers, and give them good advice. Take their interests to heart at all times and develop rapport with them so they learn to trust you.

Once your customers develop trust in you or an employee in your company, you are well on your way to turning those people into lifetime clients and passionate users. Do note, however, that trust is crucial. Offering bad advice or advice that benefits you in the short term but hurts your customers is detrimental to developing this relationship. Always have your customers' interests at heart, even if this means a short-term decrease in your profits, because it will greatly increase them in the long term. So let's look at the best ways to follow up with customers, build stronger relationships, and turn your customers into clients.

> "Once your customers develop trust in you or an employee in your company, you are well on your way to turning those people into lifetime clients and passionate users."

Objective 2: Make Yourself Available and Answer Questions

Although a phone call will always be more personal, e-mail can be a very effective tool for building relationships with your customers. If you can, be sure to answer incoming e-mails with a quality reply and quality advice. Make your e-mail address accessible. This is a great first step in building strong customer relationships. Betty in Iowa will be so surprised that the owner of the company responded to her personally that she just might tell her friends about your product. Word of mouth is priceless.

Eventually, you'll find that you just do not have enough time to respond to every e-mail and comment individually. When this happens, make sure you have a very well trained support person or support team to take over from you. Make sure they are well read and knowledgeable on the subject—as much as you are, if possible. Then, allow them to answer questions and make comments about the product, and have them do it in your name. This will continue to build strong relationships from the outset while you are off managing and strategizing.

Objective 3: Follow Up with Your Customers

To really begin to develop good relationships with your customers, try the following strategy in the beginning stages of your firm. Once per month, send a follow-up e-mail to each of the customers who have purchased from you recently. Although the interval will change depending on your product, it is always a good idea to allow a month or so for clients to evaluate your products. So if the date was June 15, for example, I would send a follow-up e-mail to all the customers who had purchased one of my products between April 15 and May 15. Adjust this to the specifics of your product. However, do not e-mail all your customers every time, just those who purchased within the interval.

You could send a follow-up something like Figure 9.2. Do note that I used the mail merge fields [firstname], [product], and [date]. These fields are stored in a spreadsheet or database for each subscriber. Using these makes it much easier to personalize each e-mail and save hours of time. You'll need to use an e-mail manager with mail merge capabilities such as iContact or Bronto to be able to use these.

I've seen this e-mail double sales totals for the day it was sent out. Much more important than this, however, is that it enables you to develop a personal relationship with your customers and continue the process of turning them into clients. The response from the e-mail will tell you how your product is performing, how your product can be improved, and what other things your customers want. This information is truly valuable. The method is also a great way to obtain wonderful testimonials. One company I used to work with collected

Subject: How is [product] doing for you?

[Firstname],

I wanted to personally thank you for purchasing [product] on [date]. How is it doing for you? Have you been pleased with the results?

Do let me know if I can answer any questions or be of any assistance.

Warm regards,
Joe Smithers, President
XYZ Corporation
joe@xyzcorp.com
1–800–242–4231

Figure 9.2 Sample follow-up e-mail.

over 250 testimonials and success stories through the use of this e-mail alone.

You may be thinking to yourself, "This can't be good. This is going to remind people about my product and increase the amount of merchandise that is returned." First of all, if you are worried about this, then you need to go back to square one and critically look at the quality and efficacy of your product. Second, in truth, yes, this follow-up may remind a few people who wanted to return your product but had forgotten. In practice, I saw that this happened with about 1 in 400 recipients who received the follow-up. However, the added lifetime value of the strengthened relationships you have built will far outweigh one or two returns. If you are confident in the quality of your product and you truly believe your product does what your sales material says it does, you should have no worries. If you do not, it will be difficult to succeed because people can always tell when salespeople do not truly believe in their products.

Creating this loop of client feedback is essential to knowing what the market wants, keeping your competitive edge, and constantly refining and improving your products. If you want to increase your market share and grow your company, obtaining and analyzing customer feedback is crucial.

So in review:

1. Instead of creating customer-to-company relationships, create client-to-person relationships. Personalize each transaction. Offer the valuable service of your advice, and take care of your customers. Decommoditize your products. Build trust and rapport and begin to turn your customers into clients.
2. Make yourself available, and make yourself open to questions. Answer e-mails and questions about orders personally or have trained support persons answer each question and provide quality advice in your name. Impress your clients with your level of sincerity and quality of advice.
3. Send out a monthly e-mail follow-up to all clients who have purchased from you between one month and two months ago. Creating this loop of feedback is essential to improving your product and knowing what your customers want; it is a powerful step in building relationships with your clients and increasing their lifetime value. Plus it is a great way to obtain testimonials. You may also want to send out a monthly e-mail newsletter with quality related content to further build rapport and trust. Use a form on your Web site to allow visitors to subscribe or unsubscribe and a program like iContact or Bronto to manage the subscribe and unsubscribe requests, send out personalized and mail-merged e-mails, and be able to obtain detailed reporting on your campaigns.

"Once you have these three practices in place, you will begin to develop strong relationships with your clients, will greatly increase their lifetime value, and will have turned fickle customers into evangelizers."

Once you have these three practices in place, you will begin to develop strong relationships with your clients, will greatly increase their lifetime value, and will have turned fickle customers into evangelizers who will encourage their friends to buy your product, too. Once you have developed strong relationships with your clients and sown the seeds of success by encouraging word of mouth, you'll be well along the path toward a million dollars in sales.

The Art of the Sale

The skill of sales is one of the most-prized attributes that an aspiring entrepreneur can have. The ability to lay out the reasons why someone should buy from you and not your competitor, in a customer-centered fashion—and then go for the sale at the exact right moment—is more difficult than you would imagine.

In your company, you may have a long or short sales cycle. You may sell a product directly to consumers via the Internet and not have to have any interaction with customers at all before they buy. Alternatively, you may be selling a service or product that costs thousands of dollars, and requires the approval of multiple departments.

You may have to present to school boards or Fortune 500 companies. It may take nine months between the time of first contact and the time the sale is closed. If your sales cycle is long, you'll have to compensate for this in your projec-

> The customer only wants to know what the product or service will do for him tomorrow. All he is interested in are his own values, his own wants, his own reality. For this reason alone, any serious attempt to state what our business is must start with the customer, his realities, his situation, his behavior, his expectations, and his values.
>
> **—Peter Drucker in**
> ***Management: Tasks,***
> ***Responsibilities, and Practices***

tions. It can become very frustrating to sell a high-ticket item or service that takes months of presentations, discussions, and contract revisions to sell.

Here are eight questions to answer to get you started on your sales plan:

1. How will the product be sold? In a retail store, online, by direct mail, by catalogs, by infomercials, through distributors, or by a combination?
2. Will you sell your product at wholesale, at retail, or both?
3. Is your main market businesses or consumers?
4. Where do customers currently go to look for the product?
5. How can we be positioned so that we're in these places?
6. Could the price point support a telesales force?
7. Could the price point support a direct sales force?
8. What is my unique selling proposition? What will make my product so different that customers will buy it rather than competing products?

Take, for example, my good friend Erik Severinghaus's former company, MainBrain, Inc. MainBrain sold Web-based school administration software that featured grade documentation and recordkeeping for teachers; the capability for parents to view the grades, tardiness, and absences of their children online; a Web-based interface for teachers and coaches to maintain a Web page for their class or sport; school closing information; event calendars; faculty and staff profiles; school message boards; and a staff directory. The software sold for between $5,000 and $25,000, depending on the requested modules and features.

The sales cycle for MainBrain was much longer than that for iContact. After MainBrain contacted a school and set up its first appointment, it could be six months until they got a signed contract. They often had to present to a school board or school administrators multiple times, negotiate the details of each contract, and then wait for funding to be available for each school or county that it sells to. IContact, on the other hand, selling Web-based software that costs between $10 and $699 a month rather than $5,000 to $25,000, has a sales cycle of less than a week in most cases, and in some cases, no sales cycle at all. Approximately half of iContact's customers sign up without ever contacting us.

I find it easier on the psyche to sell short-sales-cycle products. If you do choose to sell a more expensive product that has a longer cycle, make sure you are very good at the sales process or have a sales team that is. While iContact can rely on our Web site, frequently asked questions (FAQs) page, and free trial to make most of the sales, you will have to take an active role, experiment with direct marketing, and keep detailed follow-up spreadsheets. Either way, learning to sell is a big benefit.

> "If you do choose to sell a more expensive product that has a longer cycle, make sure you are very good at the sales process or have a sales team that is."

Even though the iContact sales team rarely goes on sales visits, each one of us has to know how to sell. For the half of our customer base that does contact us before purchasing our product, we have to know how to sell via e-mail and phone. We have to know our product inside and out, be able to answer any questions, talk on the phone with confidence, be enthusiastic, listen to the customers' needs, and emphasize our competitive advantages.

Napoleon Hill, in his book, *Succeed and Grow Rich through Persuasion,* listed 11 traits that the successful salesperson must possess. I have adapted these traits and created my own list of 9 traits that a successful salesperson must have:

1. Knowledge of merchandise
2. Belief in the merchandise or service
3. Knowledge of the prospective buyer
4. Ability to make the prospective buyer receptive
5. Ability to know the right psychological moment to close the sale
6. Initiative
7. Persistence and the ability to follow up
8. Ability to listen and respond to the customer's needs
9. A good memory

In making sales, you'll have to set certain factors such as price, return policy, warranty, length of required contract, and so on. If you are the owner of the company, try to give your salespeople a selection of things they are authorized to offer if they feel they can close the sale. For example, if the enterprise sales rep at iContact needs to close a sale, he knows that he can offer a discount up to a certain percentage to get that sale.

As far as return policies go, in nearly all cases, the longer and better your return policy is, the more money you will make in the end. Sure, if you have a lifetime guarantee you might have 1 percent of your orders returned instead of the 0.5 percent you would have had with a 30-day guarantee; however, you may also increase your sales by 50 percent.

If you are selling an item that doesn't depreciate rapidly (such as technology items) and have anything less than a 90-day guarantee, experiment for a couple months to see how much your sales would increase by offering a 90-day, or even a lifetime, guarantee. Run the numbers, and nine times out of ten you'll be way ahead of the game.

The importance of being attentive to your customers' needs cannot be emphasized enough. If sales are not taking off the way you'd like them to, it might be because—for one reason or another—you're not selling what anyone wants to buy. If you are going to become a good salesperson and a successful entrepreneur you must always keep your ear to the ground and listen to both prospects and customers. You must know what makes your customers buy and what is keeping your prospects from buying. If you can determine, and then overcome, the major buying objections of your prospects, you'll greatly increase sales—and the size of your wallet.

If you choose to sell your product online, much of your success will ride on your sales copy. If you will be writing your sales copy yourself—either for your Web site or for any marketing materials— be sure that you emphasize the benefits of your product or service and not the features. People don't care all that much that your Superturbo Lawnmower 5000 has an oversize fuel tank, autosensing cutting, and extra-sharp blades. They will care, however, when you tell them that their lawns will be cut in a third of the time without their supervision, making their lives that much easier. Always address prospects' concerns, explain how and why you are unique and better, and use persuasive devices like case studies and testimonials. If you can remember to always keep in mind the acronym AIDA, you'll be all right. Start by attracting *A*ttention. Then develop *I*nterest, create *D*esire, and spur *A*ction.

Building a Sales Compensation Plan

To be able to support your future revenue projections you will need to show how these sales will be made. If all the sales are coming through your Web site, you will only need to show your current traffic levels, rates of traffic growth, your visitor-to-customer conversion ratio, and your average sale size.

If you are selling your product to other businesses, however, via either telemarketing or direct sales, you will need a sales force and account managers who are compensated on the basis of customer acquisition and customer retention, respectively. You can view your sales force as the hunters who bring in the contracted revenue, and the account managers as the farmers who sow the relationships with clients, work to get the clients to renew the business at the end of the contract term, and advise the clients on other products or services they may need from your company.

Your sales plan and your sales compensation plan tie back into your sales coverage model, a spreadsheet that reconciles your projected revenues with the sales team and account manager count and cost. Being "at plan" refers to hitting your projected sales figures. Try to come up with a plan that has realistic sales goals, yet will require your team to stretch to hit them. To create a sales compensation plan, start by identifying and making assumptions for these variables:

- Leads generated by channel by month
- Lead-to-customer conversion ratio
- Average upfront revenue per sale
- Average ongoing monthly or annual revenue per sale
- Number of leads one sales rep can manage
- Length of the sales cycle in weeks
- Percentage sales commission paid to lead generation source (generally on contracted year one revenue), if lead generator is separate from closer

- Percentage sales commission paid to closer of the lead into a customer (generally on contracted year one revenue)
- Target new contracts per month per sales rep
- Base salary for a sales representative (usually between $30,000 and $75,000, depending on market, type of sales, commission rate, and experience)
- Number of accounts one account manager can manage
- Average up-sell revenue per client per year (sold by the account manager, above and beyond the original contract revenue)
- Percentage commission paid to the account manager on account renewals
- Target percentage of accounts that will renew each year
- Base salary for an account manager (usually between $25,000 and $40,000)

Once assumptions for these variables are in place, you can create your spreadsheet such that it outputs the following information:

- Base salary–to–commission ratio (many companies offer 50 percent base, 50 percent commission for their at-plan compensation)
- Target total annual compensation at plan for a sales representative (usually between $50,000 and $150,000, depending on market, type of sales, and experience)
- Target annual compensation at plan for an account manager (usually between $45,000 and $75,000, depending on market and experience)
- Number of sales representatives you will need to have to hit plan
- Number of account managers you will need to have to hit plan
- Revenue from sales at 75 percent of plan (worst-case projection)
- Revenue from sales at 100 percent of plan (expected-case projection)
- Revenue from sales at 125 percent of plan (best-case projection)

Building out a professional sales plan allows you to determine the breakdown in the number of people that you will need to hit the revenues you have projected as well as allowing you to share with your sales reps and account managers what you expect of them. When the time is right to build out your sales team, ensure that you have a CRM tool in place to track and manage your lead generation rates, sales funnel, sales cycle length, customer retention rates, and commission payments.

> "When the time is right to build out your sales team, ensure that you have a CRM tool in place to track and manage your lead generation rates, sales funnel, sales cycle length, customer retention rates, and commission payments."

Obtaining Publicity

Obtaining publicity is similar to obtaining free advertising, except it's better, as the advertising comes in the form of a recommendation or mention by a trusted third party. Third-party endorsements have a great deal of credibility with viewers, listeners, and readers and can generate many more leads than a paid ad.

Good media relations require planning and time, however; you cannot decide on Tuesday that you want to get a press release out by Thursday and expect to get coverage. You need to build and cultivate relationships with editors and reporters, because journalists tend to rely more on their Rolodexes than on press releases when writing their stories.

Before you launch your publicity campaign, you'll need to decide whether you'll be doing it yourself in-house or outsourcing it to a public relations firm. If you decide to hire a PR firm, you may wish to contact the business editors at local newspapers or trade journalists and ask them which firms they respect and work with often. It is also a good idea to ask for client references and have your firm present a plan with a budget and timeline. Most firms will work on a monthly retainer. It is important to keep in mind that a one- or two-month press campaign is not likely to produce results. In my experience, you will need to commit to at least a six-month spend of at least

$3,000 per month to get any results worth mentioning. If you decide to do your publicity campaign yourself, here are a few tips:

- *Know your audience.* First, know who your audience is and what types of media they pay attention to. Then build relationships with these publications and outlets.
- *Personalize your e-mails.* Instead of sending a press release directly, begin an e-mail message by saying, "I enjoyed your recent story about _____." This will improve your chances of getting noticed.
- *Become a source.* Instead of sending out a press release when you are ready to launch your campaign, send out an introduction message a few months prior to this, stating who you are and what you are an expert in. Offer to answer any questions the reporter or editor may have on these subjects.
- *Build the relationship first.* Instead of sending a press release out of nowhere, start a few weeks in advance by dropping a short e-mail to the relevant editors and reporters at your local papers, letting them know that the company will be making an announcement in the future. State that based on your knowledge of that person's work, you believe he or she is the right person to contact, and you wanted to confirm this before sending any unwanted press releases. If that person is not the right person, he or she may let you know the proper person to contact. If that person is the right one, there is a good possibility that he or she will take the chance to inquire a bit further about your company and upcoming news.
- *Create a proper media kit.* Invest time in creating a professional media kit, printed in color and presented in a nice portfolio folder. Include company information and history, product information, executive biographies, case studies, past press coverage, names of prominent clients, and high-resolution pictures of your product(s) and executives on a burned CD. Mail this kit in advance to publications or trade press that have covered stories similar to yours in the past.
- *Use resources such as Vocus, MediaMap, and Bacons to build a list of media contacts in your area,* and utilize press

release distribution services such as prweb.com, businesswire.com, and prnewswire.com.

At iContact, we executed our first campaign in the fall of 2003. Our director of marketing, Josh Carlton, created a press kit and a press release, which he mailed to the editors at newspapers in our area. We were able to get an article in the *Chapel Hill News*, through which our vice president of business development, David Roth, found us. Over time we built relationships with the editors of local publications such as the *Raleigh News & Observer, LocalTechWire, Triangle Business Journal,* and *TechJournalSouth,* so that now whenever we have an announcement it is nearly ensured that it will get coverage.

Our second campaign, in 2005, was carried out through a local firm called Maverick Endeavors. They did a good job for us, but we were not aware that we would have to stick to it for at least three months to get good results. We gave them a one-month contract for $3,000 to see what they could do, allowing them to redo our press kit but not giving them enough time to actually get coverage.

In July 2006, when iContact had grown large enough, we hired a full-time director of public relations by the name of Chuck Hester. Chuck has done a tremendous job for iContact and has gotten us countless podcast interviews and blogger reviews, placement on the cover of *Fortune Small Business Magazine* and *Success Magazine,* a mention in the *Wall Street Journal, Women's Edge Magazine,* and *CIO Magazine,* and coverage in all the local newspapers and trade journals multiple times. In my opinion, when you get to the point that you can spend $5,000 per month or more on public relations and press coverage, hire a person in-house. The in-house person's focus on your business and cost of $30 per hour, rather than the $100 per hour that a firm would charge, will get better results at a lower cost.

> "When iContact had grown large enough, we hired a full-time director of public relations."

10

STEP 8: BUILD YOUR ONLINE MARKETING STRATEGY

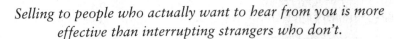

Selling to people who actually want to hear from you is more effective than interrupting strangers who don't.

—SETH GODIN, *Permission Marketing*

Over the past 10 years, I have learned a lot about Web marketing. I began in 1998 not knowing a thing about marketing on the Internet. As I have mentioned, after taking an HTML class in seventh grade, I began working with Lois, who sold pearls and wanted to sell them online. I designed her Web site, added the products to the site, integrated an online shopping cart, and started a monthly newsletter. Within several weeks, we began making a few sales. Although that business did not work out for Lois in the end, I gained invaluable experience in Web site design and learned a few lessons about online marketing in the process.

In tenth and eleventh grade, I continued to put these lessons to use in working the clients of my Web site design firm, Virante Design & Development. During this time I began reading the articles and studying the courses of some well-known online marketing experts. By the time I received that fateful call from the business owner with the nu-traceuticals product, I had gained quite a bit of knowledge about on-line marketing.

Over the next year, as we took that company from $200 a month in sales to $200,000 a month in sales, I learned more about market-ing in general and Web marketing in particular than I could have imagined. With the significant financial resources of the company be-hind me, I could try out new ideas and purchase the software I needed to be an effective Web marketer.

I learned how to effectively use coregistrations, interstitials, au-toresponders, and newsletter software. I learned how to manage a customer database and promote back-end products and special of-fers. I learned how to maximize ROI on pay-per-click engines and in-crease the lifetime value of a customer. And I learned how to get a site to the top of the search engines and how to build an affiliate pro-gram that produced an additional $45,000 each month in sales for the company. In short, the experience was again invaluable. I was 17 and had full control over a $50,000-per-month marketing budget. I learned many lessons, and through trial and error began to develop the system that I will share with you here.

Web marketing is not something many business owners are used to doing or, for that matter, very good at. However, it is something that can launch a business from nowhere to doing tens of thousands of dollars per week in sales in a matter of a few months. If you have a product that is sold to consumers or small businesses and sells for under U.S. $500, this plan is tailored to your type of business and will allow you to grow your sales without spending much up front. If you run a service-based business, this plan will help attract new customers both locally and nationally. If you run a business that sells a product that costs more than $500, the strategies described here will help you generate thousands of leads each week that your sales team can subsequently close

The system is based on five lead generation and conversion channels—techniques that have proved their efficacy time and time again in my businesses and every business I know that has properly executed them. These channels are search engine optimization (SEO), affiliate programs, permission-based e-mail marketing, cost-per-click (CPC) and cost-per-mil (CPM) advertising, and social media marketing.

Properly maximized, these five channels allow your business to be launched with very little up-front cost. They are the same channels I used at the nutraceuticals company and the same strategies we have used to position iContact as a market leader in the e-mail marketing and online communication industry. The key is executing properly and investing the needed time.

The great thing about SEO is that once you are positioned in the top of the search engines for your targeted keywords, you will receive a stream of thousands of unique, highly qualified prospects to your sites, newsletters, and autoresponders each week—all completely free of charge.

The great thing about reseller and affiliate programs is that you pay out only after a sale is made. You already have the money in your bank account before you have to write the check for the commissions, completely eliminating any risk for you.

With permission-based e-mail marketing, you can leverage the traffic on your site to obtain tens of thousands of subscribers to your newsletters, and then use software such as iContact to send out a weekly or monthly newsletter with quality content and your marketing message.

Online advertising via CPC and CPM (mil is Latin for "thousand," so this essentially means cost per 1,000 impressions) channels cost money up front to test, but if you can make either channel provide a positive return, you can greatly scale it. iContact now spends over $300,000 per month on CPC advertising alone.

Social media marketing can come in many forms, including blogging on your Web site to generate content, getting visitors to subscribe to your RSS feeds, getting other bloggers to review your product or service, participating in online forums, commenting in related communities, creating groups on social networks, creating and posting viral videos and podcasts about your business, and generating exposure for your company by creating a useful tool or controversial news. You will know you've succeeded with social media marketing when you have created interactive conversations with your customers and visitors rather than one-way broadcasts.

These strategies come down to one thing: positioning. You don't have to beat your competitors by having a better product or more money than they have—you simply have to be better positioned than they are. So let's get started with the details.

Search Engine Optimization

Search engines are the market makers of the Internet. They connect consumers with providers at the very moment of consumer interest and enable all of us to find exactly what we want, when we want it. They bring great efficiency to the Internet and our lives and will exist as long as the network of servers and computers we call the Web is around.

> "The first purpose of search engine optimization is to be positioned in the places where your customer is looking."

The first purpose of search engine optimization is to be positioned in the places where your customer is looking. The second purpose is to be positioned better than your competitors in these places. In the world of search engines, better means higher, and higher means a much greater probability that an individual will click on your link. Approximately 70 percent of users, if they click, will click on one of the first three listings in a search engine. So how do you get there?

First, you must determine which keywords you wish to target. Ask yourself which keywords a potential visitor is likely to type in when trying to find your Web site or product. Once you have determined this, work to increase the number of times this keyword or keyphrase appears on your home page. Make sure your page title contains this term and that you have lots of content on your Web site about this topic. The three most important factors in your search engine ranking are (1) the number of times your target keyword appears on your home page, (2) whether the keyword is in the title and whether you have content on your site about this topic, and (3) whether there are other, related Web sites about the same topic linking to your Web site.

The majority of Web site owners have fewer than 10 incoming links to their sites. The search engines view incoming links as verification that your site has quality content. The more related links your site has from other sites (with the underlined clickable text that includes your targeted keywords), the higher your ranking in the search engines will be. Here is a step-by-step overview of this entire SEO process:

1. *Select your keywords.* Use tools such as the Overture Search Term Suggestion Tool, Google's Search Term Suggestion Tool, and Wordtracker to determine which related keywords or key phrases it would be best to optimize your site for. Once you have a list of potential keywords, go to Google and type in those keywords. Then see how many incoming links the top few sites have. You can determine this number by typing in "link:http://www.competitordomain.com." Take a look at whether the first few sites have the targeted keyword in the domain name or in the title, or whether they appear often on their page. Use this information to estimate what it would take to get your site above the current sites in the rankings.

2. *Ensure that your site has those keywords on it.* Make sure that the keywords you are targeting are on your home page at least five times. Having a 5 percent to 15 percent keyword density for your targeted search term on your home page is optimal. Also ensure that your title tag and image alt tags contain your targeted keyword. Add your targeted term to an H1 header tag for added prominence.

3. *Build good-quality content on your site.* I call this phase the "content campaign." Either write articles yourself for the site or go through the search engines to find related content. If

you find an article on another site that you'd like to publish on your site, send an e-mail to the author, site owner, and/or publisher to request permission to syndicate the article on your site. Present it as a win/win quid pro quo in which you receive good-quality content and the author/publisher receives free exposure and a link to his or her Web site in the byline of the article. I'd suggest having at least 25 quality articles on your site before going forward. Optimize your home page for the two or three most competitive target terms. Optimize your in-site pages for the more unique and less competitive terms. You can also outsource the creation of this content to copywriters, using a service such as elance.com, for about $30 per 400-word article.

4. *Build links to your Web site.* Without incoming links to your site, it will never have a chance at being at the top of the search engines for competitive terms. Use the research you did earlier on the number of links the sites at the top of the listings have or your targeted keywords to set a goal for how many related incoming links you want to build to your own site. To obtain links, go through the search engines and find related Web sites, then contact the owners of those sites and offer to exchange links. Add their links to your Web site and e-mail them to let them know that you've linked to their sites and would appreciate a reciprocal link. I'd suggest contacting them first via e-mail and then via phone if necessary. In your initial e-mail to site owners, include the URL and description of your site, as well as the location of where their links are and which sites of theirs you are referring to. I'd suggest creating a resources section on your site and placing your link partners in the appropriate category within. You can also build links naturally through press releases or by having great content, a useful tool, a viral video, or an interesting blog. If you have more money than time, you can also purchase relevant links from quality Web sites through a service called LinkExperts or purchase

reviews with links from sites such as PayPerPost, ReviewMe, and Blogvertise. Ensure that whatever links you build to your Web site have your target key phrase in the anchor text, the words that are clickable and underlined. Finally, text links are much more valuable than image links, as the search engines can follow text links and associate the link text with your Web site, but they cannot do this for image links.

5. *Continue building your site's reputation.* Once you have built a few related incoming links, the search engines will find and index your site. If your site is new, it can take up to nine months for Google to allow it to show up for competitive search terms. During this time, continue building good-quality related content and work to build as many incoming links from related Web sites as you can.

Building a Partner Program

At iContact we have over 2,500 partners that send us visitors and customers for a 25 percent to 35 percent lifetime commission on each referred sale. We have approximately 1,300 affiliates, 150 marquee resellers, and 50 global resellers. Affiliates receive 25 percent commission. Our marquee resellers are required to sign a reseller contract but receive a higher, 30 percent commission and cobranded landing page at theirname.icontact.com. Our global resellers are companies that have more than 10,000 small business customers who can refer substantial business to us. These resellers receive a higher, 35 percent commission and special support in working with us to maximize referred sales. Approximately 15 percent of our overall sales come through our partner program, and we are working hard to grow this percentage.

Developing additional lead generation channels is an important part of growing your sales. Depending on what you are selling, a partner program may be able to help you increase your customer acquisition rates. Partner programs typically have different tiers. Affiliate partners can sign up directly on the Web site without any

> "Partner programs are essentially cost-per-acquisition (CPA) programs whereby you pay a set amount or set percentage to acquire a customer."

required review, while reseller partners often get additional benefits but must sign a reseller contract.

Partner programs are essentially cost-per-acquisition (CPA) programs whereby you pay a set amount or set percentage to acquire a customer. Once you know what your customer lifetime value is, you can easily determine the maximum amount that you are willing to spend to acquire a customer. This amount is called your maximum *customer acquisition cost* (CAC).

If you are selling a product online you can have an automated affiliate program whereby you track the exact number of referred visitors and pay a commission for any visitors who turn into paying customers. An affiliate program uses Web-based software that tracks the source of referred visitors to your site through cookies and databases, and then connects with your shopping cart to calculate commissions to the referring affiliate when a visitor they referred in the past ends up purchasing your product(s).

Affiliate programs have been very useful for Internet entrepreneurs. It seems that not a single successful online company is without one. When you launch your program, the first thing to do is obtain affiliate software. You can either purchase affiliate software like 1Shopping-Cart, AssocTrac, or MyAffiliateProgram; use an open-source platform like OSCommerce; have custom software developed; or join an affiliate network that provides both the software and the connection to advertisers who can promote your product, like CommissionJunction or LinkShare. Launching your affiliate program might cost between $1,000 and $5,000, but if you can properly build and promote your program, your return on investment will be many times this amount.

Once you've purchased the software, installed it, and ensured that it works with your shopping cart and merchant account, you'll need to decide on the level of commissions you will pay. Most programs pay between 10 percent and 35 percent of each sale. Keep in mind that the higher the rate at which you pay out, the more affiliates you will attract. However, if you are losing money on each sale, it will not matter to you how many affiliates you have.

Once your commissions are set, you'll need to create banners and images for your affiliates to use. If you are not good at graphic design, you can visit www.guru.com, www.smarterwork.com, or www.elance.com to find freelancers. You'll also need to create a guide explaining how to link to your site, and offering instructions on how to view sales statistics, a sign-up form, and sales copy encouraging affiliates to sign up. When you have done all this and tested everything, you can begin to promote your program.

To promote your program, you can follow the same general method that was used in contacting link partners. Use the search engines to find related Web sites, and contact them via e-mail and phone to encourage business owners to partner with your company. Once you have this list, contact the potential affiliates. Make sure you do it individually and customize your message for each prospect. Encourage them to learn more about your program at your site. Finally, be sure to follow up about a week later. You can also list your affiliate program on sites like Refer-It and AffiliatePrograms.com, or join a network like Share-a-Sale, CommissionJunction, or LinkShare.

Many affiliate program owners have a great affiliate program but fail to promote it. The months you are waiting for your search engine rankings to come in are a great time to promote your affiliate program. You should be able to build at least 200 to 300 affiliates during this time frame, depending on your product and the commissions you are offering. This should be enough affiliates to get a steady stream going of a few sales each day.

Once you have a couple hundred affiliates and a few months' worth of data, you can go after larger partners that can bring in $10,000 per month or more in sales. First, determine what your overall visitor-to-sale conversion rate is on your site. Using this data, figure out the average payout per visitor sent to you. If you can show empirically that it makes financial sense for larger companies to partner with you, you'll have a much easier time convincing vice presidents of marketing to take on the risk of establishing an alliance with your company and put ads for you on their site on a CPA basis.

To establish these larger alliances, you may have to increase your commission, sign contracts, guarantee minimum payouts, and get on planes. This has been the exact work that iContact's vice president of business development, David Roth, has been doing for the past four years to build our Global Reseller Partner list, and I am sure he would tell you that it is not easy but the benefits are significant to partnership building. Do whatever it takes within the realm of profitability.

In addition to a traditional affiliate and reseller program, some of the larger ad networks such as Google Adwords offer a CPA program whereby you set what you are willing to pay for a certain action (lead sign-up, whitepaper download, purchase, etc.) to occur. This can be another effective channel for acquiring customers at a predictable CAC.

Permission-Based E-mail Marketing

iContact began in 2003 as a permission-based e-mail marketing application. At the application's core, it allowed you to upload a list of contacts that had requested to receive e-mails from your organization, add a sign-up form to your Web site, select a template, paste in your content, and distribute your newsletter, then view the opens and clicks while managing the bounces and unsubscribes.

> Email marketing is fast, effective and dirt cheap—a godsend for marketers in an economy that has crunched advertising budgets.
>
> —**Lisa Takeuchi Cullen**, *Time*

Today, iContact has evolved into an online communications platform that makes it easy to create, publish, and track e-mail newsletters, surveys, autoresponders, blogs, and RSS feeds. Although RSS, blogs, and social media are becoming an increasingly important method of communication online, e-mail remains the top method of communicating with your customers and prospects.

Starting a monthly e-mail newsletter allows you to collect prospect data and stay in touch with your customers and most interested prospects. The effects of a monthly or weekly newsletter with quality content include an increased visitor-to-sales conversion rate and better brand awareness in your industry and with your customers and prospects.

The first task in starting your own e-mail newsletter is to select the e-mail list management software you'd like to use. You can choose Web-based or desktop-based software. If you want subscription and unsubscription requests and bouncebacks to be handled for you, I'd recommend Web-based software, as opposed to desktop-based software. Look for software features such as open and click-through tracking, the ability to send HTML messages, bounceback handling, unlimited list creation, multiple-message autoresponders, and message scheduling. You should also look for a tool that allows you to easily distribute your message to other channels such as RSS or blogs.

Once you select the software you'd like to use, add the sign-up form to your Web site. Most services will provide you with the HTML code you need to do this. Without a sign-up form for a newsletter on it, you are losing valuable prospect data. When visitors go to your Web site, they are often looking for a product or information that you provide. Many of these visitors are willing to sign up for a newsletter with good-quality content and more information on your industry and products.

Once you have the sign-up form posted, decide how often you'd like to send out your newsletter and the content that will appear in it, and create an information page with archives and a sign-up form on your site. Finally, log in to your newsletter software and send out your newsletter according to the schedule you decided on.

I usually send out newsletters on the same day once a month, but it is up to you how often and when your newsletters go out. As far as content, you should include at least one good-quality, substantive article in your newsletter. Intersperse recommendations for your products with case studies or testimonials. When you have completed all of this and your newsletter has been sent, add it to your archives page so new subscribers can see what past issues were like.

If you can properly execute a permission-based e-mail marketing strategy, you'll greatly improve contact and relationships with your current and future customers. You'll build your reputation in the industry and tremendously improve your visitor-to-sale conversion rate, meaning more sales, more often, for higher amounts.

> "You'll be able to build an opt-in list of thousands of subscribers within a couple years and turn these subscribers into passionate, evangelizing customers."

Especially if you can get your site to the top of the search engines, you'll be able to build an opt-in list of thousands of subscribers within a couple years and turn these subscribers into passionate, evangelizing customers. The nutraceuticals company I worked with in 2001 and 2002 was able to build a permission-based e-mail list of 30,000 within 12 months. The wonderful thing was that every time we sent out a newsletter, sales would jump by $4,000 to $6,000 that day.

iContact's company newsletter, *The Email Marketing Monthly,* is sent out on the twenty-eighth of each month. The newsletter currently has about 80,000 subscribers. Whenever we send out our monthly message, we add 50 to 60 new customers, generating about $30,000 in additional annual revenue. We're able to increase revenues by $30,000 by sending out an e-mail that would cost around $250 to send if we were paying our own prices. By implementing a similar strategy for your permission-based communications, you'll soon notice a similar impact on your bottom line.

CPC and CPM Advertising

Online advertising has a drawback. You have to pay for the ads up front (compared to lead-from-affiliate ads, for which you pay only after the customer is acquired, or leads from search engine optimization, which are free after the up-front work is done). This noted, if you can make the numbers work, online advertising through CPC and CPM impressions can be a scalable method of quickly growing your sales to the $1 million mark and beyond.

With CPC advertising, you set a maximum bid for what you are willing to pay per click, and then, based on the competition and the click-through rate on your ads, the exact cost per click is set. The major CPC ad networks at this time are Google Adwords, Yahoo! Search Marketing, and MSN AdCenter. The market share breakdown is approximately 65 percent Google, 25 percent Yahoo!, and 12 percent MSN, though there are presently some discussions about Yahoo! and MSN merging their ad networks. The second-tier CPC networks include Miva, Kanoodle, Business.com, and 7Search.

At iContact, we have scaled our online CPC spend from $15,000 per month in June 2006 to over $300,000 per month today. We scaled it in-house until we got to $150,000 in ad spend, and now we have outsourced our CPC management to a nationally known and very high-quality firm called ROI Revolution, in Raleigh, North Carolina. It is important to be able to track your advertising back to the actual sale so you can determine which campaigns are working and which are not. You can do this through a free tool like Google Analytics or through your affiliate software.

CPM advertising allows you to purchase build text and banner ad impressions at a cost per 1,000 impressions. At the time of this writing, the major CPM networks are 24/7 Real Media, Advertising.com, Tribal Fusion, aQuantive, AdBrite, and ContextWeb. You can use a tool like DoubleClick's DART for Advertisers to manage and optimize all of your ads in one location. Standard ad sizes in pixels are outlined in Table 10.1:

Table 10.1 Standard ad sizes

Type of Ad Display	Ad Size in Pixels
Banners	468 × 60
Large rectangles	336 × 280
Leaderboards	728 × 90
Inline rectangles	300 × 250
Squares	250 × 250
Skyscrapers	120 × 600
Small squares	200 × 200
Wide skyscrapers	160 × 600

Costs per 1,000 impressions generally range from $1 to $10, depending on how targeted your ads are. Run-of-network (RON) ads are generally at the lower end of the spectrum, and behaviorally targeted premium sites are at the higher end. CPM advertising is generally better at brand advertising than at generating profitable customer acquisition in the near term, but if you can make it work, you can scale quickly.

Social Media Marketing

Social media marketing revolves around creating interactive conversations with your visitors, often through new media such as blogs, videos, podcasts, and social network communities. It is a relationship, and not a promotional, form of building your brand.

Blogging can be one of the most effective ways at building quality related content for and incoming links to your Web site, as well as creating a transparent participatory discussion with your customers. You can blog using tools like Blogger, Wordpress, TypePad, and iContact. With iContact, we wanted to create a tool that allows you to blog at the same time as sending out your e-mail newsletter.

> "Blogging can be one of the most effective ways at building quality related content for and incoming links to your Web site, as well as creating a transparent participatory discussion with your customers."

A normal blog has its content in reverse chronological order with date-stamps, a commenting system, a method of tagging and categorizing posts, a method of archiving posts, and a method of subscribing to the blog's feed. Some blogs utilize a tool like Feedburner or iContact to track the number of subscribers as well as to distribute blog posts automatically as e-mail.

Most blogs show the most recent content on the home page with archives by week, category, or individual post. At the bottom of most blog posts are interactive buttons that allow users to share the post on a number of Web 2.0 services such as Digg, Facebook, iGoogle,

My Yahoo!, Reddit, Del.icio.us, StumbleUpon, Technorati, Fark, Furl, Ma.gnolia, Newsvine, Slashdot, Spurl, and TailRank.

Blogs can also utilize widgets that allow additional interactivity by showing information such as the avatars of the community members (MyBlogLog), recent videos (YouTube), photostreams (Flickr), slideshows (RockYou), bookmarks (Del.icio.us), favorite blogs (called a blogroll), favorite music (Last.fm), social network updates (Facebook, LinkedIn, MySpace), what the blogger is currently reading (Goodreads), and what the blogger is currently doing (Twitter). Other forms of social media marketing include the following:

- Creating a community of your users through an off-site social network like Ning, Facebook, or MySpace, or an on-site installed tool like Drupal, Shark, OneSite, CommunityZero, or CommunityServer.
- Creating a presence in a virtual world such as SecondLife. (Yes, this is being done.)
- Creating a unique or controversial story and submitting it for exposure on Digg and Netscape.com.
- Claiming your blog and building up a reputation for it on Technorati.
- Exchanging blogroll links with other related bloggers.
- Adding a discussion forum to your site.
- Participating in online forums that discuss your field.
- Adding information about your company on Squidoo, ZoomInfo, or Wikipedia (if it is noteworthy enough, that is).
- Creating interesting videos showing what you do and posting them on video-sharing sites such as YouTube and MetaCafe.
- Creating podcasts and then distributing them via iTunes and Odeo.

By means these methods, you can go from being a company that communicates via a one-way broadcast tool into a company that builds authentic open dialogue in a democratic, participatory manner.

Bringing It All Together

Let's quickly review your Web marketing plan in step-by-step form.

Phase One: Get Your Site to the Top of the Search Engines

1. Select your keywords.
2. Ensure that your site has those keywords on it.
3. Build good-quality content on your site.
4. Build links to your Web site.
5. Continue building your site's reputation.

Phase Two: Get Hundreds of Affiliate Web Sites to Promote Your Product

1. Purchase affiliate software.
2. Install affiliate software and connect with a shopping cart.
3. Decide on a commission rate.
4. Create an affiliate central with statistics, images, and linking instructions.
5. Create a sign-up form and sales copy.
6. Contact potential affiliates—this phase will take the longest.
7. Send out a monthly newsletter to affiliates that incorporates best practices and stories of successful affiliates.
8. Mail out checks on a monthly basis to affiliates who have made sales.
9. Build a reseller program of larger partners.
10. Understand your conversion rates and average commission, and then pitch larger potential partners by showing them in advance what they can expect.

Phase Three: Turn Your Prospects into Lifetime Customers with a Regular E-mail Newsletter

1. Sign up for Web-based e-mail list management and marketing software such as iContact.
2. Add a sign-up form to your Web site to begin collecting the information on prospects.

3. Send out a daily, weekly, or monthly newsletter to stay in touch with your subscribers, provide quality content, recommend your product(s), and tell of successes with your product.

Phase Four: Test and Then Scale CPC and CPM Advertising to Grow Sales

1. Sign up for accounts with Google Adwords, Yahoo! Search Marketing, and MSN AdCenter.
2. Set up a tracking system with your affiliate program or Google Analytics so you can track the exact return from your ad spend.
3. Bid on keywords on each of the networks.
4. Adjust your bids depending on performance.
5. Test new match types, geographic targets, landing pages, and ad copy to maximize the return and scale your spending while maintaining the same customer acquisition cost.
6. Generate a few graphical creatives in the standard sizes.
7. Do a tracked test on one of the major ad networks: 24/7 Real Media, Advertising.com, Tribal Fusion, aQuantive, AdBrite, or ContextWeb.
8. If the test is profitable, scale it.

Phase Five: Create a Transparent Discussion with Your Customers Using Social Media

1. Add a blog to your Web site using Blogger, Wordpress, TypePad, or iContact to build related content and incoming links.
2. Post to your blog often.
3. Utilize Feedburner or iContact to track your RSS feed subscribers and automatically send e-mail updates to them.
4. Utilize Technorati, Squidoo, Wikipedia, MyBlogLog, Del.icio.us, Zoominfo, iTunes, Odeo, Digg, and Netscape. com to get more exposure for your social media content.
5. Utilize off-site social networks like Facebook, Ning, and MySpace or on-site social network applications like Drupal,

Shark, OneSite, CommunityZero, and CommunityServer to build an interactive community of your customers.

6. Participate in online forums and comment on blogs that discuss your field.

Now that we have the full five-phase plan in place, let's show how all the channels interact to produce a winning Web marketing strategy. Figure 10.1 summarizes the relationships and flow of traffic.

In essence, the search engines provide traffic to your site, which converts visitors to prospective clients with product recommendations and obtains their contact information with an autoresponder e-course and free e-mail newsletter. You continuously stay in touch

Figure 10.1 Your $1 million Web marketing flowchart.

The 20 Keys to Online Marketing

Following are 20 keys to successfully marketing your product, service, and business online.

1. Have a professional, easy-to-navigate, quick-loading design. Hire a professional design firm or at least use a good site template.
2. Have lots of quality related content.
3. Build lots of links to your Web site.
4. Build credibility and rapport.
5. Start an e-mail newsletter with quality content and send it out at least once per month.
6. If you are selling a product, have an affiliate program.
7. Once you have an affiliate program, don't forget to promote it.
8. Do whatever you can do profitably to attract large affiliates and form key strategic alliances.
9. Position yourself advantageously in the search engines.
10. Use cost-per-click (CPC) engines, but make sure you know the lifetime value (LTV) of your customers and that you do return-on-investment (ROI) checks often.
11. Supplement your affiliate advertising with both online and traditional advertising, but track results and always do ROI checks.
12. Advertise using CPM channels to build brand recognition, but put profitability before brand recognition.
13. Offer yourself as a resource to the media as an expert in your niche.
14. Hire a great publicity firm or bring an experienced publicist in-house.
15. Use autoresponders to maintain constant contact with prospective customers.
16. Remember that business is all about relationships and communication. Always work to build more relationships, and once they are built, make sure you are in continuous contact

with your prospects, customers, strategic alliances, suppliers, investors, and the media.

17. Encourage word of mouth among your customers.
18. Have superior customer service and have staff to answer all incoming e-mails within 24 hours.
19. Send out periodic e-mail follow-ups making sure your customers are happy and asking them for feedback on your product and the service your company has provided.
20. Blog frequently with quality content.

Reprinted from www.zeromillion.com with permission.

with your prospects and customers with your e-mail newsletter, blog, and RSS feed, building your reputation as an industry leader. Through this process, highly qualified leads are generated for the product site, which is also receiving traffic from the affiliate program and your CPC and CPM ads. Your product site is optimized to convert visitors to prospects, prospects to customers, and then customers to lifetime customers with whom you can build an organic and transparent interactive dialogue.

11

STEP 9: BUILD YOUR TEAM

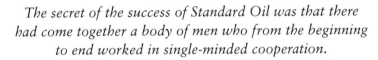

The secret of the success of Standard Oil was that there had come together a body of men who from the beginning to end worked in single-minded cooperation.

— JOHN D. ROCKEFELLER

How to Build Your Team

You've spent months and perhaps years of hard work getting your business to the point where you are nearly ready to make your first sale. You've developed your business idea, closed on deals with suppliers, ordered your inventory of products, written your business plan, incorporated, and raised the money you need to get started. Before you can truly begin to grow quickly, you'll have to build your team and infrastructure, and put a few key systems into place. When you can afford to bring your first employee on, do so. If you never hire anyone, you'll be doing all the work yourself, which means you are creating a job rather than building a business.

Many aspiring entrepreneurs have asked me how to find a business partner. I always answer that a partner is not someone you can find overnight or in a few weeks. It usually can only be someone with whom you have been friends for a while and in whom you have developed and established trust—someone who has worked for you for some time or someone you've worked with in the past.

The skills of my business partner, Aaron Houghton, complemented mine. Aaron is a tremendous programmer and technologist, while my core skills are in marketing and building a company. We were able to work together to create something greater than either of us could have created separately.

Having a business partner can be helpful in various ways. Partners can help with financing, with industry contacts, or in taking over roles with which you have less experience. They can allow you to get twice the work done in half the time and give you that needed motivation when things are tough. If you wish to find a partner, start networking. Join your local Chamber of Commerce and volunteer for committees and in your community. If you are a student, join business clubs or business fraternities. Talk to people about your business whenever you can. Put up flyers looking for a partner in an entrepreneurial business. If you receive any replies, meet with those people and, if you feel it would be good to do so, start your chosen candidate in a role where the person can begin to learn and demonstrate his or her commitment. After a few months, you may be ready to offer the person part ownership in your company.

> "One of the toughest conversations to have with your partners is the discussion regarding equity distribution. But it is a necessary conversation to have up front."

I have found that one of the toughest conversations to have with your partners is the discussion regarding equity distribution—the percentage of ownership that each partner will get. But it is a necessary conversation to have up front. It is often hard to negotiate with someone who is a close friend of yours. Because of this, some partners simply decide to split things equally. Unfortunately, it is a rare occurrence that all persons involved contribute equally to a company. If the proper steps are not taken, this type of situation—when one partner does not keep up his or her end of the deal—can destroy a long-lasting friendship.

To prevent this situation from occurring, I highly recommend two things. First, no matter how difficult it is, have a serious conversation with your partner(s) about who should get what. Base your discussion on the following four factors:

1. Work completed in the past
2. Monetary investment in the company
3. Who will be doing work in the future
4. Experience and contacts in the industry

Second, I'd very much recommend vesting your shares and having a stock restriction agreement. Vesting is the granting of ownership over time, instead of all at once. For example, if you give a partner 30 percent of your company without vesting his or her shares and the partner leaves a month later, he or she will leave with 30 percent. On the other hand, if you vest that partner's shares over three years, he or she will leave with only 0.83 percent of the company. In this case, the partner would have to work for the full three years to receive the 30 percent. Vesting is used often by venture capital companies to put "golden handcuffs" on top executives. If you do use vesting, you'll need to have a stock restriction agreement that spells out these terms, including the terms of sale and transfer.

Before you launch your company, you may wish to bring additional persons, such as industry veterans or key investors, onto your board of directors. Simply keep in mind that you should have an odd number of board members at all times, as decisions cannot always be made with an even number since a majority vote is needed and an even number of board members can result in a tie. In order to attract experienced people to your board, you may need to offer stock options or a yearly stipend for members. You also may wish to set up an informal advisory board for your company.

As your company grows, you will have to add certain professionals and outside advisors to your team. You should have a good accountant, attorney, financial advisor, insurance agent, and banker. These important advisors will be a big part of your company's success or failure. As Robert Kiyosaki and Sharon Lechter say in *Rich Dad's Guide to Investing*, "First dream of having a team of full-time accountants and attorneys. Then you can have the big boat and the free time."

As you grow your team and begin hiring employees, you'll have to quickly learn to evaluate applicants and resumes, and do interviews. I evaluate the two most important qualities that a good worker can have—initiative and work ethic. You'll quickly learn that no matter what someone's experience, if you can find someone who has a bias toward action, takes initiative, and has a solid work ethic, you'll have found someone whom you'll want on your team permanently.

Originally, I conducted all interviews for iContact. Today, the director of human resources screens the applicants, and the manager within the relevant department conducts the first interview. If the manager wishes to submit the candidate as a possible hire, I will then interview the person. The manager ensures the applicant is qualified, has the needed experience and capabilities, is able to start the position within a reasonable time period, and accepts the salary range we are offering. Generally, I am simply checking to make sure the applicant is sane, has a good work ethic, and can communicate well. At the risk of giving a slight edge to future applicants who read this book, my favorite interview questions to ask are as follows:

1. Tell me about yourself? Where are you from and what is your passion in life? (You can't ask where a person lives, but you can ask where the person is from.)
2. Tell me about what you did at your last position.
3. Why are you no longer at your last job? Or why do you wish to leave?
4. What have been your failures and the mistakes that you've made in life?
5. What adjectives would you use to describe yourself?
6. What are a couple experiences in your life that have changed you and made you who you are today?
7. What were the most difficult periods of your life?
8. How did that experience change you?
9. As an individual, what are the things that you believe in?
10. Are you familiar with what this company does?
11. How would you describe what we do?

12. What are your favorite books?
13. What do you like to do outside of work?
14. What are the goals that you have for your professional life?
15. What are the goals that you have outside of your career?
16. What do you see yourself doing in three years?

This company has grown very quickly since we started out with two employees in a 700-square-foot office in Chapel Hill. We now have over 80 employees and 25,000 square feet of office space in Durham.

We have employed interns from UNC, NC State, and Duke as we needed to in the marketing, development, and systems administration departments. We hired the best team we were able to assemble and used job boards such as Monster, HotJobs, TriangleJobs.com, LinkedIn, and Craigslist; local networking groups such as RTP 2.0, the Triangle Linux Users Group, Triangle Internet Workers, and Triangle PHP Users Group; local university career centers; and social networking tools like Facebook and LinkedIn to spread the word about the positions.

After raising the seed round of funding in May 2006, we began to use recruiting firms such as HireNetworks, The Select Group, and FullScale Solutions to fill positions. These recruiting firms charge us between 10 percent and 15 percent of a placed employee's first-year salary as their fee. This cost can be between $3,000 and $10,000, depending on the salary and rate, so it can get expensive quickly.

Setting Priorities as a Manager

As your company grows and you assume the role of a manager, you'll need to gain new skills. You'll need to learn how to manage people, delegate responsibility, identify leaders, and set priorities. Here is a simple model that can be used to assist in setting your priorities.

Whether you are planning out a long-term strategy or setting priorities in the midst of a crisis, the model shown in Figure 11.1 can

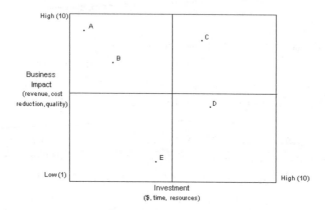

Figure 11.1 Business Impact and Investment Priority Setting Model.

help you order the tasks or projects that should be done first. To use the model, simply plot on the vertical axis the impact each project will have on your business, and on the horizontal axis plot the amount of money, time, and resources it will take. Do this for each project you must prioritize.

As you can see, projects that are plotted closer to the top left are those that you should pursue first. They are the ones that will have a big impact on your business without costing much to implement. In this example, you would aim to complete project A first. This same model can be used to prioritize any type of to-do list and assist you as a manager in ensuring that your time is being spent in ways that will most benefit your business.

There have been days over the past five years when I have felt as though everything was on fire and a model like this would have been of no use whatsoever to me. On a day-to-day basis, I use Outlook 2007 and a legal notepad to keep notes. I put an A with a circle around it next to any task that is an action item, and I meet at least three times a week with our executive assistant, Michelle Tabares. Michelle helps maintain the list of ongoing projects and tasks that I need to get done, as well as transcribing voice mails, writing correspondence, booking travel, and filling out purchase orders and reimbursement forms for the director team.

10 Management Lessons

Over the past five years, as iContact and Virante have grown, I've learned a lot about managing people. A business amounts to little without the people behind it. As I mentioned in the section on building a team, the two most important things I look for when hiring are initiative and work ethic. I cannot overestimate the importance to the eventual success of your business of bringing on good people. But once you have hired these good people, how do you manage them?

I certainly admit that I have much left to learn about leadership and management, but here are a few tips that might be helpful:

- *Have a vision and communicate it.* Make sure you clearly communicate your vision for the company. No one follows a leader who cannot communicate the way in which the company will succeed. The future of all your employees is tied closely to the success of your company. Make sure they believe in your company, what it stands for, and its products and services, and make sure they know that the hard work they are putting in now will pay off.
- *Show respect.* Treat people, including your customers, suppliers, partners, and employees, with respect at all times.
- *Share your success.* Make sure your employees share in the success of your company. As the company is able, provide additional benefits such as health care and dental coverage, a stock options plan, and a 401(k) plan. As your employees' skills and abilities grow, reward them with fair compensation. Finally, consider incentivizing your top employees and managers with ownership in the company. Few things can make a person work harder than a piece of the action.
- *Don't be too serious.* Make the business environment fun at times. While being professional and taking things seriously is important, nothing can beat the effects of a companywide midnight round of bowling after you reach an important milestone, a lunchtime pizza party once a month, or a spontaneous Nerf-dart duel.

- *Work with your employees.* Make sure the employees see you there and working with them. No one likes to work hard for someone who doesn't work hard him- or herself. Especially early on, be the first to arrive and the last to leave whenever possible.
- *Keep your door open.* Whether or not you have your own office yet, keep your "door" open. Make sure your employees and managers know that you are approachable at any time about any problem they are having.
- *Listen.* You have built a great team and are paying top dollar for it. Hold meetings with your management team at least every other week. Also have frequent informal ad hoc discussions with your partners, managers, and employees. Get their feedback, discuss the business and its strategy, and inquire every so often if there is anything that is frustrating them that you can help with. A few weeks ago I had a quick spur-of-the-moment meeting with the lead developer for iContact. After inquiring whether he had any job frustrations, it came out that he felt he was working in an environment in which he became distracted too often. We quickly devised a solution whereby he would work at home four hours a day until we could move into a larger office where the development team could work in a separate room, away from the distraction of the sales and support team. This small change has doubled the developer's productivity.
- *Build relationships.* Without understanding at least the basics of what is occurring in an employee's out-of-office life, it can be hard to connect with the person on a professional level. One tactic I've used successfully to get to know each employee personally is to take the person and his or her significant other to dinner the first evening of their employment. It serves as a way to celebrate the occasion as well as learn a little bit about the employee that would not come out in interviews or through reading a resume.
- *Commend more than you criticize.* Too many business owners (and I have been guilty of this as well) speak to an

employee only when he or she has done something wrong or something that has negatively affected the company. While constructive criticism and appropriate guidance have their place, if you seem to only condemn and never praise, your employees will quickly either dislike you or show apathy toward their jobs. Continual properly placed praises can be as powerful in getting quality results from employees as a large pay raise. Many people thrive on peer and superior recognition just as much as on money. Instituting an employee-of-the-month award and a quarterly performance review can be extremely valuable to your company.

- *Consciously build a culture.* At iContact, we truly are a family. In fact, we call ourselves the iContact Family. When someone is moving into a new house or needs a ride home from the airport, we're there to help. We believe in building people up, not tearing people down. We put people first and have respect for the individual. We believe that we should work hard and be innovative, yet maintain a balance in our lives. We believe in not letting balls drop, and that we're all working together on the same mission. We have foosball and Ping-Pong tables in our office, free sodas, Bagel Monday, and monthly birthday celebrations and Outstanding Performance Award ceremonies. We have a young, dynamic, fun, and innovative culture. It exists because we have consciously built it.

As a manager and business owner, you are charged with an immense responsibility. You control the activity and purpose that your employees dedicate half of their waking hours to. Make your company's purpose meaningful, communicate your vision, respect and praise your employees, and share your success. If you can succeed in building a team of highly motivated and happy employees who take initiative, have a bias toward action, respect you, and truly care

> "Make your company's purpose meaningful, communicate your vision, respect and praise your employees, and share your success."

for the business, you will have done much of the work toward building a strong and fast-growing organization.

Fighting Bureaucracy

Although systems are necessary in building a successful company,
these systems must be efficient and built upon processes that can be
instituted throughout the organization without bottlenecks or inefficiency. Proactive empowerment is a management theory that I developed out of need and that I use to help reduce bureaucracy within an
organization. It is a methodology through which individuals are empowered to know they are in charge of and perform at their peak
while completing certain projects within an organization.

iContact generally has 30 to 40 unique projects going on at any
one time. Prior to implementing proactive empowerment, I was generally aware of what the projects were. We had a weekly director
meeting at which I could get an update and ask questions. However,
I would find myself asking questions only when the topic of discussion triggered the question. I had no systematic way of knowing what
projects to follow up on to ensure that they were on track and moving forward.

One night I sat down and listed all the projects that were going on
in the company; there were 36 of them. Next to each one I listed who
was leading that project as well as the other people who were working on it. It turned out that a lot of projects had people working on
them but no one in charge of them.

The problem that we were encountering as an organization was
that people who were supposedly leading projects but who weren't
on the management team did not feel empowered to do whatever
they had to do to complete the projects. Because they did not know
they were leading the projects, they did not know they had the
authority to figure out how to get the resources necessary to achieve
their objective.

Since I wasn't doing anything to *block* the projects from happen-
ing, I wondered why they weren't getting completed. At the same time,
when the people working on a particular project ran into one road-

block, they would assume it was management who was stopping it from progressing. In most cases, people were simply busy and needed additional reminders from the project leaders.

Over the next week I sat down with the people involved in each of the 36 company projects. I made sure there was a clear leader for each and told them, "I want you to be proactively empowered to work on this and do whatever you need to do within the organization to make things happen and reach this defined goal." Once the project leaders knew that they were in charge and had authority vested in them to navigate the waters to get to a conclusion, projects were executed more effectively and a lot more quickly.

A lot of time the mentality among employees outside of management is that if there is an obstacle, it's not their fault or they don't need to anything about it until they hear more about it. In many cases it really is not the team members' fault, but as the result of proactive empowerment, they now know it is their responsibility to figure out how to solve the problem. The nonmanagement project leaders were externalizing the situation by contending that they couldn't do anything about certain issues because they were not in management; they would simply send in a ticket and wait until they heard back from management, rather than proactively tracking down the cause of the inefficiency and following up on it. Proactive empowerment provided an effective method for resolving this impasse.

As a very specific example, our director of customer support, Amber Neil, needed a CRM tool to better track the statistics concerning incoming tickets for customer support for iContact. The tool cost $249. Amber knew she needed this tool to do her job effectively, but she wasn't in charge of the software budget and she didn't do anything about it for three weeks or so. Finally, one day she mentioned to me that it would be great if she had this software. I responded that as a director she does not need to fill out purchase orders for items under $300. Although the policy had been in place for a few months, she had not realized she had purchase order authority to acquire whatever she needed for her department up to the $300 limit without having to get the approval of upper management.

In this case, if I had told Amber in advance, "Here's the project I want you to work on, here is the goal, and here are the people you are working with; do whatever you need to do to get this done," she would have resolved the situation much more quickly.

Instead of reactively authorizing team members to proceed and having work become bottlenecked when it gets to me or another director, I now write a project brief at the start of any project. Then I proactively say to the team leader for that project, "This is what we are trying to accomplish. You are authorized to do whatever you need to do to get this done." Projects now proceed much more efficiently.

To summarize, the first phase of proactive empowerment is to identify the project. The second phase is to identify the people who will work on the project and the leader. The third phase is to provide the brief to the project team and project leader and ensure that the leader knows that he or she has the authority to do what is needed to accomplish the task.

35 Lessons I Have Learned

At the end of each year, I post on my blog the most important lessons I learned that year. Here are the major lessons I've learned over the past few years.

1. *The people with whom you surround yourself matter.*
   Venture capitalist Steve Nelson shared some advice with me this year, and it has stuck with me: "Stay involved with only the best. Ask yourself—are these outstanding people? To know, you only need to ask yourself: do they possess great intelligence, keen business insight, outstanding people skills, and unquestioned integrity?"
2. *Life reveals the rules only after you start playing.* Life is a game, and it's one that doesn't exactly reveal most of the rules until you've been playing it for a while. There are two ways to figure out the rules: either talk to smart people who have already done what you're trying to accomplish or use trial and error. Either way, start playing early.

3. *Judging people is necessary.* As a child, you learn never to judge people. The very phrase "judging people" perhaps has a bad connotation. But in business, you must judge, and you must judge often. You must judge based on intelligence, on effort, and, more important, on results. If you don't judge, you end up with unexamined, unmeasured mediocrity. All humans have equal inherent value, but not all humans' productive efforts are equal.

4. *If somebody sues you, talk to them in person.* I spent about $35,000 unnecessarily in 2006 by listening to my lawyer and not communicating with a former client who was taking Virante into arbitration. If I just would have flown out to meet him in person at the start instead of four months later at the mediation hearing, I likely would have saved that $35,000 and a lot of personal stress. The lawyer's advice was correct and proper legally, but the legal solution often costs a lot of money to get to.

5. *Build consensus with the core before you present widely.* Build preemptive support and communicate your vision individually to your executive or director team, or in small groups, to get feedback and make adjustments before presenting to everyone. This can be a lot of work, but it's how things should be done in companies larger than 20 people.

6. *Life is too short to not be passionate about what you do.* Stand out, make an impact, be compassionate, and help others. Too much injustice occurs in this world to not want to make a positive change at whatever level you can. Torture, human slavery, murder, genocide, starvation. Too many people don't have the opportunities we have, and too many people die needlessly from preventable diseases and starvation to make you not want to do the absolute best you can in your life. Have fun. Enjoy life. Help others. Reduce suffering. That is the credo.

7. *"Yes, and" life.* One of the key lessons of improvisational acting is to say yes to the scene that your acting partner is

creating. If your partner suggests that you're kissing cousins in a ski lodge, then you are kissing cousins in a ski lodge *and* something else. By saying "yes, and" in response to people instead of "no, but," you often create better outcomes and build a much stronger relationship with the person you're interacting with.

8. *There are four must-attend conferences for future leaders.* In June 2006 I sat next to John McCain and talked about soccer and energy policy as we watched the semifinal of the World Cup for 15 minutes. I had a conversation with Madeleine Albright about security and aid policy in Africa. I talked about digital camera technology while riding on a bus next to Steve Jurvetson on the way to Michael Eisner's ranch. I sat next to Glenn Close, Sandra Day O'Conner, and Stelios Ioannou, of easyJet fame, in a roundtable discussion on climate change. How'd I get there? Five years of consistent hard work and getting invited to attend a conference called Fortune Brainstorm. Getting invited to and attending a few key conferences can give you access to pretty much anybody in the world. In my experience so far, those key conferences are Fortune Brainstorm, the World Economic Forum, TED (Technology, Entertainment, Design), and the Clinton Global Initiative Annual Meeting.

9. *There's a good deal of corruption in the world—it can affect policy—and competition can reduce it.* In 1995, the telecom companies had the technology to launch DSL. But they held off for nearly five years. Why? Because the cable companies didn't yet have the technology ready to launch cable modems and the telephone monopolies saw hundreds of millions of dollars of second-line dial-up revenue from their subscriber base. Instead of providing DSL to Americans and allowing economic-enhancing broadband access, they (somewhat understandably perhaps) held back the technology to make more money, in the meantime using their huge lobbying base to ensure that government policy wasn't enacted that would benefit all other businesses, all consumers, and the entire

economy. Finally, in 1999. the technology for cable modems became ready and marketable, and amazingly, DSL launched. The lesson is that business in general and consumers in general should have the right to lobby and influence, but a single industry should never have the power to lobby at the expense of the wider good.

10. *Compounding experience and compounding resources allow for greatness over time.* The big wooden flywheel from Jim Collins's *Good to Great* has held true in my business experience. It takes a long time to get the flywheel moving at all. It takes a lot of really hard pushes to get it going. Each individual push doesn't move it very much. But if you keep pushing, eventually the wheel starts moving and momentum starts to take over, causing each subsequent push of equal strength to have a greater and greater impact. In 2003, iContact did $12,000 in sales. In 2004, $296,000. In 2005, $1.3 million. And in 2006, $2.9 million. We worked from October 2002 until December 2003 to generate $12,000 in sales (and $20,000 in expenses!). We worked equally as hard in 2006 as we did in 2003, but instead of $12,000 we generated $2.9 million with the same effort. Intelligent, consistent effort compounds as experience, knowledge, and access expand. Sometimes it is difficult to fathom how people like John D. Rockefeller, Andrew Carnegie, and J. P. Morgan acquired their fortunes and made the impact they did in one lifetime. They started by working their butts off to make $12,000, and 40 years later they were working with hundreds of millions of dollars. Same way Warren Buffett did it, same way Bill Gates did it. Play life like a long-term game. And always keep improving.

11. *Networking isn't about handing out business cards.* In every personal development conference you attend, you hear that networking is key to business success. And that is, in fact, true. But most teachers leave out the most important rule of networking. It's not about shaking hands, engaging in a little small talk, and swapping business cards. It's about

building real, trusting, mutually giving relationships with quality people.

12. *The world has a lot of problems, but they are mostly fixable,* One of the reasons I want to be a U.S. senator one day is to be able to influence foreign policy, especially the policy that deals with how our country interacts with other countries from an economic and environmental standpoint. This year, I've been made so consciously aware of the extreme inequities in the world today. Over 2.7 billion people live on less than $2 per day and 49,000 people die every day from preventable disease and starvation. Most people don't have the opportunity to be creative through entrepreneurship because of class divisions and bureaucratic restriction. The developed nations produce an unnecessarily large amount of greenhouse gas, causing agricultural famine in nondeveloped nations. Billions of dollars go to farm subsidies in the United States and the European Union, allowing silos of grain to be wasted while millions die of starvation due to lack of access to markets in developing nations. I have been deeply affected by these issues and hope to dedicate much of my life to improving these situations on a global scale through politics, business, and social entrepreneurship.

13. *Community matters.* For every thought I have about Malawi, Benin, or Burundi, I think about my home of North Carolina. For every issue in Malawi, Benin, and Burundi, I can see a parallel issue (though on a different scale) here in North Carolina. The lesson: although you should always educate yourself about the world, what happens in it, and how you can make a global difference, you can most often make the largest difference right at home—and there are always plenty of issues (read: opportunities to improve) right here in our own community.

14. *Be aware of that little voice.* Listen to that little voice in the back of your head. It's usually alerting you to something that might come back to bite you if you don't listen to it.

15. *Communicate.* Don't let noncommunication lead to the degeneration of a relationship. Don't be passive-aggressive. Attack issues immediately and head-on.

16. *You eventually have to balance the bias toward action.* Full-on bias toward action is great. But only when you have little to lose. Once you have something to lose, you must balance having a bias toward action with analysis, due diligence, and care.

17. *Face the day.* Don't avoid doing things just because they are hard or may cause conflict.

18. *Find and eliminate bottlenecks.* Consistently look for bottlenecks and inefficiencies in communication flows and organizational behavior, and eliminate them.

19. *Know what matters.* Integrity is what matters at the end of the day. There will always eventually be an audit or a lawsuit that has to investigate what you're doing right now. So make sure at all times that your actions are above board and in good faith.

20. *Business can be harsh.* The business world can be harsh, and oftentimes there is someone in your life whom you trust that you should not and who will eventually try to take advantage of you.

21. *Avoid going around a manager.* If there is a layer of management between you, as CEO, and the person you need to address, speak to that person's manager first to make sure it is okay to proceed, or just relay the message through that person's manager. To avoid priority conflicts, avoid assigning work to people you do not directly manage. Rather, in all cases except emergencies, give the task to the person's manager to assign.

22. *Know the value of praise.* As motivating factors, recognition and praise can be just as important to employees as salary and bonuses.

23. *Hiring takes more time than you think.* Finding the right people when you need them is a significant challenge and can take longer than you would think.

24. *Communicate openly with your customers.* Always communicate openly, fully, and quickly with your customers during any negative events.

25. *QA is important.* Quality assurance is a critical part of the software development process. Don't release a new version of your product until it has been thoroughly tested by both an in-house QA team and a subset of your customer base. Bugs that make it into a released version are much more costly both in lost sales and in loss of brand goodwill than spending the money needed to fix them up front.

26. *Raising money takes time.* Raising funding for a company will take longer than you expect.

27. *Prepare when things are going well.* It is better to prepare for the worst when things are going well rather than when they're not.

28. *Sometimes you have to set them free.* Sometimes you just have to let go. Get the right people, train them, and then trust them. Trust, but verify.

29. *Communicate your vision often.* Just because you have a detailed plan in your head doesn't mean other members of your team know it. If you don't consistently communicate your vision and plans, people may think you don't have vision and have failed to plan.

30. *Be nice to she who decides your credit limit.* Be very nice to merchant account processing limit review officers and give them the information they need to review your limit well before you hit it.

31. *Be accessible to your employees and clients.* Reiterate whenever you can that you are available for any employee to speak with. Have lunch with every member of your team (in cross-departmental groups of three to four people) at least once a year. Publish your e-mail address and phone number for your clients. You can always delegate a client request or problem that comes to you via e-mail or voice mail—but at least you will be aware of it.

32. *Let your managers know when you go outside to learn.* If you're going to discuss a topic or department with someone outside the company in order to get information for yourself, but you already have someone in charge of that area in-house, either include the manager of that area in the discussion or alert the manager in advance that you are seeking information from an outside source. This prevents your managers from suspecting that you are trying to replace them, make them irrelevant, or marginalize them.

33. *Don't undersell yourself.* The world has a lot of opportunities to grow. If you keep working hard, you will meet people and learn new methods for growing your business and your sales. In the fall of 2005, I probably undersold the company to potential investors, saying we were the third-largest e-mail marketing company trying to become the first and then sell for $25 million to $30 million. I should have said, even if I didn't yet know how we'd accomplish the goal, that our target was to become the leading provider of online communication software and become a public company with an exit of $250 million or more. I didn't yet believe in that vision at that time, but I should have.

34. *Randomly tell people that they are doing a great job.* As busy entrepreneurs, we don't tell our employees that we appreciate them enough. Tell them they are doing a great job at least once a quarter, if not more often.

35. *Don't accelerate in the snow without tread on your tires.* Make sure the right underlying processes, systems, and people are in place whenever possible before you attempt to rapidly scale the business.

12

STEP 10: BUILD STRONG SYSTEMS AND SCALE

*Achievement comes to someone when he is able to do great things
for himself. Success comes when he empowers followers
to do great things with him. Significance comes when
he develops leaders to do great things for him.
But legacy is created only when a person puts his organization
into the position to do great things without him.*

—JOHN C. MAXWELL

Creating Systems and Automating Operations

As your business grows, you will need to build systems and processes and attempt to automate as much as you can. You'll need to build distribution systems, inventory systems, marketing systems, follow-up systems, customer support systems, research and development systems, accounting systems, and hiring systems, among many others. Systems are formalized rules, policies, and procedures that trained individuals can repeat as your company expands. iContact has document systems for human resources (HR), accounting, employee train-

"Systems are formalized rules, policies, and procedures that trained individuals can repeat as your company expands."

ing, billing, product development, marketing, sales, management, technical operations, and account management.

From the start-up of your business, as you create each system, document the details, as well as any general business rules and procedures, in an employee handbook. This book will become invaluable as time progresses. iContact's Employee Handbook currently consists of 38 pages containing background information on the company, founders' biographies, lists of the officers and the members of the board of directors, a company description, a description of our main product, frequently asked questions about our product, a company timeline, an overview of agreements, and office procedures and policies including those covering the following issues:

- Adverse weather
- Attendance
- Backup
- Change of information
- Commission
- Confidentiality
- Deliverability
- Disaster recovery
- Downtime notification
- Dress code
- Drugs
- Food
- Freelancing
- Holidays
- Job responsibilities
- Large sender acceptance
- Maternity leave
- Network usage
- New employee training

- Parking
- Paternity leave
- Payroll
- Performance evaluations
- Phone answering
- Phone usage
- Printing
- Product development
- Quality assurance
- Reimbursement
- Server installation
- Sexual harassment
- Vacation
- Voice mail
- Workers' compensation

As we grow the business and things change, we continuously add to the handbook. A number of forms have also been developed at the company, although we try to keep these to a minimum. We use forms for the following activities:

- Purchase orders
- Travel requests
- New-hire requests
- Expense reports
- Creative briefs
- Client proposals
- Health insurance enrollment
- Dental insurance enrollment
- Paid leave requests
- Written reprimands
- Verbal reprimands
- 401(k) beneficiary
- Employment eligibility I9
- Supervisor reviews
- Employee reviews

- Letter stationary
- Envelope stationary
- Employee offers
- Confidentiality contracts
- Nondisclosure agreements
- W4 tax deductions
- Flexible spending account (FSA) plan enrollment
- Vacation requests
- Job descriptions
- Direct deposit setup
- Workout room liability waiver
- Database modifications
- Fax cover sheets
- Affiliate thank-you letter
- Collections letter
- Invoices
- Customer support templates

We utilize a number of spreadsheets in the organization, including the following:

- Board package
- Monthly billing records
- Purchase order records
- Cost-per-click (CPC) return on investment (ROI) reports
- Operations plan
- Annual budget
- Profit-and-loss statement
- Chargeback record
- Depreciation schedule
- Development timeline
- Product feature requests
- Personnel directory
- Balance sheet
- Accounts receivable
- Affiliate check records

- Revenue projections
- Sales compensation plan
- Large sender pricing

Our weekly director report provides a wealth of key information, including the following:

Support Metrics
- Percentage of abandoned calls
- Average hold time
- Average call duration
- Calls per day
- Calls per 10-minute interval
- Customer contact by type
- Calls per week
- Total time on phone
- Total hold time
- Number of abandoned calls
- Number of chats
- Total time in chat
- Average chat duration
- Number of e-mail tickets
- E-mail ticket response time
- Tickets/chats/calls per rep

Billing Metrics
- Weekly sales figures
- Attempted transactions
- Successful transactions
- Declined transactions
- Check and wire sales
- Credit card sales
- Amount credited
- Overdue accounts
- Amount of accounts receivable
- Number of accounts receivable

Marketing Metrics
- Total visits
- Total pageviews
- Average pageviews per visit
- Average time on site
- Percentage of new visits
- Bounce rate
- Total trials
- Total full accounts
- Trial to full conversion
- Visitor to trial conversion

Product Development Metrics
- Bugs reported
- Bugs resolved
- Maintenance tickets opened
- Maintenance tickets resolved
- Systems tickets opened
- Systems tickets resolved
- Percentage of stories completed
- E-mail sending speed

Sales Metrics
- Closed customers by rep
- Revenue by rep
- Total closed
- Total new revenue

Finally, our management dashboard provides real-time information on the following:

- Number of paying customers
- Number of overdue customers
- Monthly paying customers
- Annual paying customers
- Customers by plan type
- Number of trial customers

- Number of affiliates
- Total sales to date
- Accounts receivable total
- Monthly reorder revenue
- Annual reorder revenue
- Yearly revenue
- Monthly revenue per customer
- Average length of a customer relationship
- Customer lifetime value
- Renewed accounts by month
- Trial to full conversion percentage
- Annual revenue by month
- New annual clients by month
- New customers by month
- Net new customers by month
- Cancellations by month
- Retention percentage by month
- Revenue per customer by month
- E-mails sent per month
- Added revenue per month
- Lost revenue per month
- Net new revenue per month
- New trial users by month
- Monthly trial to full conversion

All of these systems, procedures, policies, metrics, forms, and reports have evolved over the past four years out of necessity to be able to better manage the business. Always remember that investors do not like to invest in systems that go home at night. If you can build proper systems so that your business will operate properly whether or not you are there to oversee it, your business will grow faster and be much easier to sell. Although it takes longer to set up the system for a task than to do a task yourself, in the long run you can save a lot of your time and effort by setting up the system.

Building your company from a new business into an enduring organization causes some growing pains. Creating an employee handbook can't help with all of these. You'll also need to do payroll, ensure

Action Item 6: What Systems Will Your Company Need?

Take a moment to write down any systems or procedures that you will need to develop for your company.

_____

_____

_____

compliance with human resources laws and regulations, create automated reporting mechanisms, and ensure that your books are up to high standards. Here are four specific lessons I've learned that are related to the process of establishing systems and procedures:

1. It's best to outsource your payroll. Figuring out state tax, Social Security, Medicare, FICA, and unemployment amounts and making sure exact payments are made on time can be quite a hassle if you choose to do it yourself. We use a company called Paychex to handle cutting checks for employees and paying all applicable state and federal payroll taxes.

2. Be sure to establish a procedure for hiring new employees. All new iContact employees must sign employment, confidentiality, nondisclosure, and noncompete agreements. They also receive a direct deposit enrollment form, a W-4 form, a health insurance enrollment form, and an employee handbook.

3. Maintain records relating to personnel and performance to protect yourself against lawsuits related to employee termination. Conduct quarterly evaluations of each employee yourself until you are large enough to have a full HR department.

4. Hire a good accounting firm and establish an appropriate accounting procedure. At iContact, we keep all of our financial records and receipts for each month and then mail them to our accounting firm at the beginning of the next month. They input the records into QuickBooks Professional and then mail the files back to us. We get a monthly profit-and-loss statement and balance sheet. The same firm also handles our yearly taxes.

As you go from being a small start-up to an international player in your industry, you'll have to manage the operations of a number of activities. In all cases, focus on creating efficiency and optimizing every operation. The more you can automate your operations, the better. If you can properly navigate the process of creating systems, develop an employee handbook, deal with payroll and HR, establish an accounting process, and focus on efficiency, you'll be well on your way to turning your new business into an enduring company.

For a case study on operational efficiency, check out www.ryanallis.com/operations-efficiency.html.

Selecting Office Space

Behind every successful business there are systems, processes, and infrastructure. We'll talk about building your systems and processes later. For now, let's focus on infrastructure. By infrastructure I mean everything in your business that must be set up for your business to run. It includes things like Internet connections, phone lines, phone systems, computer networks, product liability insurance, and office space. Let's take a minute to review a few tips on how to select good office space.

In my business experience, I have been fortunate to always be able to find good space in which to conduct my business. When I was a computer consultant as an adolescent, I worked on location at the client's place of business or residence, and thus did not need an office. As a Web site designer when I was 15 and 16, I worked out of my room in my parents' house. It had a hand-painted black desk covered with pictures of my friends and places where I had been. It was a great place to get work done and enabled me to save up quite a bit of money.

The first office I ever worked in was that of the nutraceuticals company I worked with in 2001 and 2002. The space was on the second floor of a building, above an air-conditioning company, and had a very useful freight elevator—essential for taking the large shipments of product up to our storage closet. The owner negotiated a very good deal on the place, as he purchased an extended lease while the place was in disrepair—and then paid a few hundred dollars to have it cleaned, painted, and recarpeted.

When I moved to North Carolina, I did not have an office for a couple months. I worked out of my sixth-floor dorm room in the Ehringhaus Residence Hall. By October, however, I had met Aaron Houghton through the Carolina Entrepreneurship Club and he allowed me to use his 700-square-foot downtown Chapel Hill office space at no charge. After we incorporated iContact in July 2003, he continued to allow us to use the space at a discounted rent. As I mentioned in Chapter 1, this office had all of the necessary facilities including a T1 line for Internet access, a wireless office network, cable TV, a George Foreman grill, a bathroom, a love seat, a coffeemaker, a top-of-the-line phone system, a large conference room, and three workrooms.

Now that the company has grown to 10 employees, we have decided to move to a larger office space a few miles away. We'll be moving into this 2,300-square-foot space this September. In our search we've had to take into account factors such as cost per square foot, upfit costs, property taxes, telecommunication providers, proximity for employees, and the contract length (usually three or five years). We hired an office space broker to negotiate on our behalf.

Before you begin your own search for office space, you'll have to determine what you will need. Will you need a storefront retail location, a large storage warehouse, a high-profile location to impress visiting clients, or simply a room in a shared office building? A commercial real estate broker can help you answer these questions, provide strategic advice, and find properties that fit your needs. The service of your broker is paid for by a commission from your monthly rent, which would be the same price regardless, so their services are effectively free.

Once you determine what you'll need, take a look in your local classified section to see what office space is available in the area. When you locate a potential location, your broker will set up an appointment with the owner or agent. When evaluating potential locations, take into account the number of square feet, location, parking availability, broadband options, room arrangement, storage space, whether the complex has a receptionist for all the tenants, amount of security deposit, and average monthly utility bills.

When you do settle on a place, you'll likely have to get the electricity turned on, purchase general business liability insurance, call the DSL or cable company to get a site survey done for Internet access availability, and head to the office store to pick up some furniture and supplies. Before you begin furnishing the office, you might wish to take a picture of your empty office. I still have the picture of the empty office I walked into in June 2003 that would become iContact. It's a magical experience to see that empty office—all your dreams, goals, and plans to build your company into one will soon fill that room and, later, something much larger.

Creating Your Accounting System

Before you begin doing much business, it will be of great benefit to get your accounting system in order. Many businesses fail because of improper financial controls and reporting. Because proper cash flow management is such an important key to building a successful business, it is imperative to always know how much cash you have on hand, what your expenses are, and what liabilities and assets the company has at any point.

The basis of your accounting system are your journal entries, income statement, balance sheet, and cash flow statement. Your income statement keeps track of your revenues and expenses; your balance sheet tells you the value of your assets, liabilities, and owners' equity at any point in time; and your cash flow statement allows you to monitor the flow of money to and from your business over any set period.

You can use software such as QuickBooks, Quicken Business, or Money Small Business to make managing these financials yourself much easier. Before iContact was large enough to have a dedicated bookkeeper, I used QuickBooks, and all I had to do was import the bank statement once a month for each of my companies and categorize each transaction. The software automatically generated my balance sheet, income statement, and cash flow statement. Today, we outsource our bookkeeping activities to a nearby firm. We simply drop off our bank and credit card statements along with our receipts and paid invoices at the beginning of each month, and the firm categorizes them and provides us with updated financial reports as we require them.

When you hire your first employee, you'll have to set up a payroll system. Essentially, this allows you to keep track of what you pay your employees and ensure that you pay the FICA Social Security tax each quarter to the IRS and the state if you are in the United States. It is much easier if people work for you as independent contractors and you can send them an IRS Form 1099 at the end of the year to document their earnings. If people are working for you full-time, you'll have to add them as employees. At iContact we have decided to outsource this payroll responsibility to a company called Paychex. They simply call us twice per month to get the payment figures and then they process the payment, withhold the proper taxes, and direct-deposit the appropriate amount in each employee's bank account.

Once a few months' worth of transactions have appeared in your accounting software, you can use the reporting features to examine the ratios calculated for your business. These ratios are similar to a report card for the business. They'll quickly tell the experienced businessperson or investor how your company is doing. The most common ratios are the quick ratio, the current ratio, and the debt-to-equity ratio.

Quick Ratio (Acid Test) = Cash + Receivables/Total Current Liabilities

The higher your quick ratio is, the better. The more available cash and receivables you have and the fewer the liabilities, the better off you will be. Your liquid assets should always be greater than your current liabilities. The higher this ratio is, the longer your company will be able to stay afloat if your sales revenue dries up. This ratio should be at least 1. The quick ratio is also known as the acid test, because it offers a quick look into the health of a company.

Current Ratio = Total Current Assets/Total Current Liabilities

The current ratio confirms whether your business has enough current assets to meet the payment of its current debts, with a safety net for possible losses in current assets, such as inventory reductions or collectable accounts. A ratio of 2 or higher is considered acceptable.

Debt-to-Equity Ratio = Debt/Equity

To find your debt-to-equity ratio, simply divide the amount of debt you have by the value of the owners' equity in the company. Try to keep this number close to zero. While debt can be beneficial if used correctly, a debt-to-equity ratio higher than 1 may indicate that you have too many liabilities for the amount of value in your company, creating the potential for bankruptcy.

Focusing on Building Your Business

As a business owner, you should also look at inventory turnover, gross margin ratio, net margin ratio, accounts receivable turnover, return on assets, return on equity, and return on investment. These ratios are very useful in managing your business. And always remember: cash flow is king. If things ever get too complex, that's an encouraging sign—because at that point you're likely making a good amount of money and can afford to hire a chief financial officer.

As soon as you can afford it, hire a qualified bookkeeper and, later on, a CFO. You might also hire an accountant to help you set up a payroll system and file the company tax return each year. Having people in these capacities on your team allows you to focus on building your business rather than making journal entries.

Scaling Your Business

There are a few main methods of scaling your business. You can:

- Invest more in online or offline advertising
- Open up offices in other cities and countries
- Create distribution partnerships with firms in other locations
- Franchise your company
- Raise additional debt or equity capital to expand
- Expand your sales team
- Bring on additional management or board talent
- Sell part or all of your company to a larger company or private equity firm that can help you expand

Regardless of the methods you choose, if you have the right systems in place beforehand, your life will be much easier. Never accelerate in the snow without tread on your tires. As you build and scale your company, ask yourself this key question: will your business be able to make money while you sleep? All highly successful businesses do.

Doing Business Internationally

By the time I left the nutraceuticals company I worked with in high school, the company's main product was being sold in over 30 countries. The company had retailers in many of those countries; however, most of the international orders came from individual consumers. It was gratifying to know that the company's marketing message was getting out to people in Malaysia, Chile, and Uzbekistan. That's what top placement in the search engines and a large network of affiliates can do for you.

Learning how the customs systems of individual countries work was an interesting experience for me. Sometimes it would take shipments sent via the U.S. Postal Service more than four weeks to arrive in Canada. Customs often opened the packages and inspected them before sending them on. Strangely, we found that if we shipped via FedEx, packages got through in one week instead of four. Even stranger, packages would arrive in Kuala Lumpur, Malaysia, in four days—quicker than most packages to Toronto.

As your company begins to open up a sales channel to international markets, you will need to do research on the specific regulations and customs agencies of each country you wish to expand to. There are many strange regulations, tariffs, and taxes that you'll encounter when doing business overseas. Each country seems to have a different policy.

Depending on the type of product your company sells, you may need to develop product packaging and labeling in different languages. You may also want to establish distributorships with stores in that country or hire local sales representatives who know an area to represent your firm and products. You can also look into the possibility of setting up subsidiaries of your company in each country or establishing official partnerships or joint ventures with existing companies. No matter how you do it, you cannot overlook the international market. If you play it right, sales outside of your own country will soon grow to exceed those within it.

Creating an Operating Plan for a Growing Company

The business plan pro forma projections may be all that are required to get a loan or satisfy an angel or seed-round investor. However, once your business has substantial revenue you will need to provide more detail about it, convert your accounting system to a format that adheres to generally accepted accounting principles (GAAP), have your accountant provide accrual-based statements, and provide a model that ties together your sales pipeline, customer acquisition rates, marketing spend, and capital expenditures in a more detailed format.

At this point, a full operating plan and model are needed. Within an existing organization, a board of directors often talks about "the plan." They may ask, "Are we at plan or above it? Is the 'plan' flexible enough to adjust for a new strategic direction and revenue model?" The plan that is being referred to here is the company's board-approved *operating plan.*

The operating plan is developed annually, and quarterly updates are provided by the CFO with help from the CEO. These are often needed to raise a second round of funding or a round above $1 million. The operating plan in many cases is a massive spreadsheet workbook that contains multiple sheets that tie together the growth assumptions, the revenue projections, the GAAP category expenses, the R&D, the capital expenditure, the cost of goods sold (COGS), and the marketing spend and relate these variables to the employee head count and the budget.

The operating plan for iContact includes the components discussed here. Note that iContact is now a company with over 70 employees and $10 million in annual sales; you will likely not need as comprehensive a model to effectively run your business when you are starting up. Knowing how this model is created may be helpful, however.

iContact's operating plan has evolved greatly since the very experienced CFO was hired in March 2006. Originally, I simply had a cash-basis budget with revenues projected for three years and expenses projected for one year, with an upcoming-year P&L. Today, the plan is built and managed by Tim, the current CFO; Lisa, the accounting manager; Robert, the director of financial operations; and Desmond, the accounting intern. The plan incorporates all of the following components.

Revenue Tab

1. Revenue projections for the next three to five years, broken down by month, driven by adjustable variables such as customer growth per month, customer retention, and average revenue per user (APRU).
2. Historical revenue by month since company inception.
3. Revenue (broken into subcategories of revenue by product

line, unrecognized revenue, chargebacks, returns, cash-basis revenue, and GAAP revenue).
4. Plan revenue versus actual revenue historical comparison with percentage of variance.
5. A sales plan with compensation detail for your sales team (hunters with compensation tied to client acquisition) and account managers (farmers with compensation tied to client retention) that drives your revenue projections.

Expenses Tab
1. Past and projected expenses in GAAP summary format (COGS, sales and marketing, R&D, general, and administrative).
2. Past and projected expenses broken down into major expense area category by month (administration, labor cost, marketing, travel and entertainment, professional fees, rent, communications, hosting, depreciation, and interest), with subcategories as needed.
3. Plan expenses versus actual expenses historical comparison with percentage of variance by category and subcategory.
4. Cost of goods sold calculation information that shows which expenses and head count feeds into COGS.
5. A benefits detail sheet that lists which employees receive what benefits, what each benefit cost is, and who pays for which benefits.

Head Count Tab
1. Head count adds and subtractions historically per month.
2. Projected head count adds for the next three to five years by department by month, with projected compensations, tying directly into labor costs on expense and P&L tabs.
3. Analysis of average company revenue per employee and average salary per head count.
4. Breakout of existing head count by department with name, title, and salary.

Statement of Operations (P&L) Tab

1. Projected revenue summary by month.
2. Projected operating expenses broken down into major expense area categories by month.
3. Operating income by month.
4. Any nonoperating expenses such as depreciation and interest expenses.
5. Net income by month, historical and projected.
6. Earnings before interest, taxes, depreciation, and amortization (EBITDA) by month, historical and projected.
7. Historical revenue, expenses by category, and net income for each year the company has existed.
8. Forward-looking P&L for upcoming one to two years based on projected revenues and projected expenses.

Balance Tab

1. Expenditures by category for capital items budget (servers, computers, phones, hosting, software, furniture) feeding directly into the capital expenditure line on the P&L and depreciation schedule.
2. Depreciation schedule with list of all physical and technical assets, their purchase value, and the length over which you've chosen to amortize their value.

Cash Flow Tab

1. This section combines the GAAP income or loss from the statement of operations, with the changes in working capital, capital expenditures, long-term debt, and equity from the balance sheet to arrive at the net cash flow for the company each month.
2. If the difference is negative, then the company is burning cash and it is important to know the average cash burn over the most recent months divided into your checkbook balance (cash position) for the company. The result gives you the number of months remaining before the company needs to have additional money coming in.

Together, these sheets make up the plan. Essentially, the goal of the plan is to model your business in spreadsheet format, which makes the job of a financial manager, an operations manager, or an investor doing due diligence easier.

Being *at plan* simply means that you've hit your revenue, cash flow, and net profit projections. Being *above plan* means you've exceeded your revenue, cash flow, and net profit projections. Being *below plan* means you've underperformed based on your revenue, cash flow, and net profit projections.

Are Your Projections Too High, Too Low, or Just Right?

The CEO and CFO often have multiple factors influencing the plan that they submit for approval by the board of directors and sometimes the investors. They do not want the revenue projection to be too high, or else they will look like they underperformed as leaders; if the projection is too far off, it might appear as if the company does not have enough money in the bank to sustain operations. They also don't want the projection to appear to be too low, for then they will (1) fail to motivate their team with an easy plan to hit and be perceived as leaving growth on the table and (2) receive a lower valuation in any financing rounds from investors who are basing part of the valuation on the plan. Submitting a revenue projection plan that is known to be low so as to improve performance perception is called *sandbagging*.

Overall, the incentives tend to balance where CEOs and CFOs submit scenarios that they expect to be able to hit with 50 percent confidence, identifying some risks on the downside and opportunities on the upside.

In reality, most venture-backed companies are below plan most of the time, though they all, of course, shoot to be above it. This occurrence is likely due to the short-term incentive to publish higher revenue projections in a venture-backed company to get a higher premoney valuation in a funding round because of perceived higher future revenues and profits.

Some less-than-forthright venture firms tend to encourage this practice, preferring that the CEO publish unreachable revenue targets so that they have an argument for obtaining additional control within an organization. In extreme situations, this can force a down-round of capital to be raised, which means that the funds are raised at a valuation lower than that of the prior round (which in turn does all kinds of nasty things to existing common shareholders).

In an ideal situation, as a venture-backed CEO you will have to neither sandbag nor overshoot. If you can show 100 percent annual growth, knowing you'll actually hit this target and perhaps exceed it, few people will accuse you of sandbagging, and two to three years of a sustained history of exceeding the plan will do wonders for your premoney valuation and ability to control the terms of the deal.

Review of the 100 Most Important Steps

I am a believer in the value of step-by-step guides as well as reviews of the most pertinent material. In this section, I'll review the 100 most important steps in building a company to $1 million in sales. Note that the following steps may not be in the exact order followed by and may not apply to every type of business. However, the general sequence remains approximately accurate, and the majority of steps will likely apply to your business.

1. Come up with a business idea.
2. Use the MAR Model of Opportunity Evaluation to assess that idea and determine whether it is a true business opportunity.
3. Research suppliers of your product.
4. Determine if what you can charge for the product will cover the cost of producing it plus an ample markup.
5. Talk to potential customers and evaluate whether you will be able to sell your product.
6. Determine a name for your company.
7. Write a business plan.
8. Complete your pro forma income statement.

9. Determine how much you'll need to raise to get your business to cash flow positive—the point where you are making more than you are spending.
10. Get feedback on and improve your business plan. Go to your local chapter of the Service Corps of Retired Executives and review your plan with them.
11. Determine your financing strategy. Determine where you will raise any needed funds.
12. Determine who will own what percentage of the company.
13. File your articles or certificate of incorporation with your secretary of state. Incorporate as a limited liability company, an S corporation, or a C corporation if you are located in the United States. You can incorporate yourself, using an online service, or use your law firm.
14. Obtain an employer identification number (EIN) from the Internal Revenue Service so you can open a bank account and hire employees.
15. File Form 2553 with the Internal Revenue Service if you intend to be an S corporation.
16. Select a corporate law firm in your area that is accustomed to working with entrepreneurial companies like yours.
17. Have your law firm create nondisclosure, noncompete, and confidentiality agreements, and have everyone involved with your company sign them.
18. Hold your initial board of directors meeting and sign the organizational consent document.
19. Decide whether you want to have a stock options plan and create an options pool.
20. Discuss whether you wish to use vesting (granting equity to the founders over time based on how long they stay with the company and what they do). If you decide to vest, have your law firm write a stock restriction agreement, have everyone involved in your company sign a copy, and then have each person consider filing an 83(b) election if you are located in the United States.

21. Issue stock certificates.

22. Have your law firm draft consulting agreements for any independent contractors and employment agreements for any employees. Get these agreements signed.

23. Open and fund a bank account, put in any initial contributed capital, and order checks.

24. If you decide you'll need to raise money, look into the different sources of money, including debt capital from family, friends, or the bank or equity capital from accredited private investors or venture capital firms. If you think you can start out small, bootstrap, and grow organically from revenues, evaluate whether you wish to grow your company in this manner.

25. If you decide you'll need to raise the money from private investors, have your law firm work with you to refine your business plan and connect you with potential investors. You may need to figure out how to develop your product and start making at least some revenue before investors will take you seriously.

26. Raise the money you will need.

27. Apply for a credit line at your bank as well as several company credit cards.

28. Purchase small business accounting software such as QuickBooks and keep track of all expenses and revenue, or hire an accounting firm to take care of this for you. You also may wish to outsource your payroll.

29. Come up with (a) name(s) for your product(s).

30. Trademark the names of all your product(s).

31. Trademark the name of your company.

32. Develop your product(s), if you will be selling a product. Ask for quotes from different suppliers.

33. Have a logo created.

34. Either purchase or lease office space.

35. Furnish your office with desks, chairs, couches, filing cabinets, and light fixtures.

36. Purchase any needed office supplies.

37. Purchase any software you will need.
38. Call your phone company and have them install a phone line or purchase a VOIP system.
39. Purchase phones.
40. Obtain broadband Internet access and a wireless router and set up a wireless office network.
41. Determine the roles with which you need additional help and can afford to pay someone to fill, then hire people for those positions.
42. Obtain general liability insurance and any other types of insurance you may need.
43. Have business cards made.
44. Have letterhead stationery made.
45. Have a brochure and any needed sales collateral designed.
46. Design the packaging and labeling for your products.
47. Have the labeling reviewed by your lawyer.
48. Print enough labels and packaging for the initial production run.
49. Obtain a Universal Product Code (UPC) bar code if you will be selling your product in stores or to retailers.
50. Order an initial inventory of products.
51. Have professional pictures of your product(s) completed.
52. Register the domain name for your company Web site and product site(s).
53. Obtain hosting for your Web sites.
54. Design your company Web site.
55. Make sure you have traffic analysis software such as Google Analytics installed on your site and check your visitor count and traffic details often.
56. Add sales copy to your Web site that is written to attract attention, generate interest, establish credibility, create desire, and provoke action.
57. Install a shopping cart on your Web site.
58. Apply for a merchant account so you can accept credit cards on your Web site and in your business or sign up with a service such as PayPal or ClickBank. If you are a service-

based company, and will be paid via checks, there will be no need to apply for a merchant account. Start doing business right away, making sure to always leave extra business cards with clients in order to leverage word of mouth. You may also want to purchase an ad in the local phone book.

59. Sign up with an e-mail list management service such as iContact and add a newsletter sign-up form on your Web site.

60. Sign up for an autoresponder service and add an eight-day informational e-course in order to generate leads, build trust with customers, and recommend your product.

61. Add content to your Web site. Ask others for permission to syndicate their content and write a few articles yourself to start to portray yourself as an expert in your industry.

62. Optimize your Web site for the search engines.

63. Build related links to your Web site.

64. Add a discussion forum and blog to your site.

65. Once the merchant account is approved, obtain a gateway such as VeriSign or Authorize.net and connect it to your shopping cart or point-of-sale terminal.

66. Install an autobill/continuity program and integrate it with your merchant account, shopping cart, and affiliate program. Decide on what type of incentive you will give to those who sign up for the autobill program.

67. Decide what your money-back guarantee will be.

68. Decide what you will charge for shipping if applicable.

69. Create a mission statement and corporate values statement for your company. Consciously build the culture of your company from the beginning.

70. Hire any needed employees before you start selling.

71. *Start selling!*

72. Sign up for a live-person chat so customers on your Web site can chat with your customer support team.

73. Install a CRM system to manage your customer interactions and sales funnel.

74. Consider starting a contest or sweepstakes for your product in order to obtain additional prospect data and leads.
75. Utilize your blog and other forms of social media like videos and podcasts to gain more exposure for your product or service, and start a conversation with your customers.
76. Investigate regulatory issues in other countries and determine which countries you can export your product to.
77. If you are selling a product, hire someone to fulfill orders or use a fulfillment house.
78. Establish relations with local media.
79. Write and mail out a press release to local newspaper, radio, and television media or hire a public relations firm to handle this for you.
80. Start an affiliate program. Install your affiliate program software and decide what commissions you will pay on referred sales. Go through the search engines and trade journals to find potential affiliates. Contact the potential affiliates in person or via phone, mail, or e-mail.
81. Build a few hundred affiliates that promote your product(s) for a percentage of each sale. Mail the commission checks to your affiliates each month.
82. Start sending out your monthly e-mail newsletter to those who signed up on your Web site and to your customers.
83. Follow up with your customers once a month to ask how they are doing with your product. Ask for and add testimonials to your Web site and marketing materials.
84. Look into upcoming trade shows and attend them. Consider creating a booth and exhibiting at and/or sponsoring any especially important shows for your industry.
85. Once you have some data on your visitor-to-sale conversion rate and the amount affiliates are paid per visitor sent to your site, work on building strategic alliances with larger partners.
86. Consider establishing a wholesale price for your product and looking for distributors of it.

87. If you decide to offer your product via stores, design and create point-of-sale items such as a display case and print collateral.
88. Take a look at the operations of your company and see what areas you can make more automated or more efficient.
89. Bring on a bookkeeper to handle your accounting work for you if you have not already.
90. You may wish to create an employee benefits program if you have not already, to ensure that you retain your most valuable workers.
91. Write a company handbook and online wiki and begin to establish formal systems and processes. Make things efficient and try not to overload workers with forms and red tape.
92. Once you become cash flow positive, look into paying for CPC and CPM newsletter coregistration; print, radio, or television advertising; or advertising via direct mail. Keep a close watch on return on investment at all times.
93. If your product(s) fit the proper criteria, look into creating an infomercial to promote them. Look into sponsoring athletes or related events or providing your product to high-profile people free of charge.
94. Allocate some funding for research and development and attempt to develop additional products.
95. If appropriate for what you are selling, develop a sales compensation plan and build out a sales force for your product.
96. Create an operations plan that ties together your revenue projections with your expenses, head count, and capital expenditures.
97. Hold a retreat at least once a year at which you and your managers discuss any issues and brainstorm on how to grow the business.
98. Build out the first layer of management within your company and hire a director of human resources and executive assistant when you are able.

99. Now that you have revenue, go to the bank and expand the size of your credit line.
100. Consider raising investment capital more seriously now that you have some revenue and scaling the business.

Congratulations! You now have a business doing over $1 million in annual sales. Depending on the revenue multiple your company is valued at (usually between 1× and 6×) and the amount of ownership you've retained, you may personally be a millionaire on paper now. There is a long way between being a paper millionaire and being an actual millionaire, however. Keep focused on building a great product or providing a world-class service, creating good jobs, giving back to your community, scaling ad spend with a positive return, creating needed systems and processes to ensure efficiency, and hiring great people, and you will make it.

Although building a company to $1 million in sales is a worthy goal, the end goal for many is either a sustainable cash-flowing organization that can provide ongoing dividends to shareholders or an exit event that may take quite a few years longer to reach. It is important to keep in mind that a company can exit in just four ways:

1. Get bought by the general public by having an initial public offering
2. Get bought by or merge with another company
3. Have an orderly shutdown in which all creditors and employees are paid
4. Go bankrupt

Beyond the $1 Million Level

If you've been able to create a successful company with paying customers, an in-demand product, an experienced team, and solid systems, you'll be well on the road to reaching the $1 million mark in sales. Once you reach this level, your business will begin to take on a much different character than the one it had when you started up. Your systems will begin to reach full stride and, depending on your profit margins, you may be able to do things such as hire a large sales force, a team of MBAs, and experienced industry executives; spend on research and development; and execute national print and media advertising campaigns.

You'll have much easier access to the credit you might need for further expansion and you'll be in a position to gain the respect of larger companies, enabling you to create more and more profitable joint ventures. You'll be able to join the Entrepreneurs' Organization, if you are under age 40, and put money into spinning off other ventures. You'll be able to start thinking about selling your company or putting the plans and people in place to shoot at a public offering in another three to four years—or continue to enjoy a good income from profits each year if you prefer to keep the company as a lifestyle business. Congratulations, you have made it!

Okay, if you haven't actually made it yet and have just been reading this whole time, at least you can visualize it. The first step toward achieving a goal is being able to visualize it.

Part Three

★

CHOOSING TO BE SUCCESSFUL

13

STEPS FOR SUCCESS

It is not the critic who counts. . . . The credit belongs to the man who is actually in the arena; whose face is marred by dust and sweat and blood; who strives valiantly . . . who, at the best, knows in the end the triumph of high achievement; and who, at the worst, if he fails, at least fails while daring greatly.

—THEODORE ROOSEVELT, 1910

Having a Bias toward Action

In my experience, prior to being able to become a successful entrepreneur, there are some important concepts to study. These include having a bias toward action, knowing how to frame failure, building relationships, and having a positive attitude. Let's discuss one of the more important principles—having a bias toward action.

Too often, someone will have a goal, yet never get going on the path toward reaching it. Many aspiring entrepreneurs have a business idea, yet spend months and months writing the business plan in a state of analysis paralysis—never taking action. If you are going to be a successful entrepreneur, however, you must have a bias toward action.

In my speaking engagements, I illustrate this principle with an anecdote. Imagine yourself at your house, and you want to go to your friend's house four miles away. You do not want to leave until all the traffic lights on the way are green. Of course, it is clear that you will never leave. This paralysis happens to many in everyday life. If you want to get there, however, you must get going now. Yes, there will be stop signs and red lights along the way, but you'll get through them—and you'll make it to your friend's house eventually, which you would not if you had waited for all the lights to be green along the way.

You can drive from Los Angeles to New York, traveling only at night and being able to see only 200 feet ahead of you at any given time. Yet you can make it, seeing only part of the journey at a time. Just because you cannot yet see the path toward a goal, don't not make that goal. To be successful, you must first define what success means to you. You have to start with a goal in mind, perhaps even a big hairy audacious goal (BHAG). Once you've defined your goal, you can get started on it. Have a bias toward action and get going. You may not know all the steps or the problems and challenges you'll run into just yet, but that is okay.

As you progress toward your goal, you will continue faster and faster up the learning curve. You'll gather momentum and as you move forward you'll gain new knowledge and, just as important, build new relationships, which will be very important in helping you reach your goal. As the momentum snowballs exponentially, your new knowledge and new contacts will create new possibilities and opportunities, allowing you, with persistence, to reach your goal.

To take advantage of this principle of accelerating momentum, however, you must cultivate a bias toward action. To initiate the momentum, you must act. Once those first small accomplishments begin falling into place, momentum will take over as these new possibilities propel you up the learning curve closer and closer to your goal. Every important goal you reach is preceded by thousands of actions without which you would not have had the opportunity, contacts, or knowledge to accomplish the final important achievement.

On Failure and Learning from Mistakes

Most people are afraid to fail. They worry constantly about not living up to expectations, about making a mistake, or about trying something new. Because of this, many never get started on the path toward reaching their goals, and thus they assure themselves of the very thing they are afraid of—failure. In order to become a successful entrepreneur, you will likely have to pay your dues. You will likely fail a few times, learn your lessons, and only then be able to come through a winner. While you don't have to take wild chances, you do have to take calculated and educated risks.

In the world of academics, mistakes are perceived as bad and something to be avoided. Throughout your school days, you are taught that mistakes are bad and embarrassing—when, in fact, mistakes are simply opportunities to learn something new. The more mistakes people make, the more they will learn and the greater the chance they will have of succeeding on their next try. The key, however, is to learn from your mistakes and avoid making the same mistake twice.

Thomas Edison would never have invented the lightbulb if he did not take this principle to heart. Edison "failed" 6,634 times before he found a filament that would create light for a sustained period of time. He did not view these as failures, however. On the 6,635th try to find a workable filament for the lightbulb, Edison did not see himself has having failed 6,634 times. He reframed the situation so that, to him, he had successfully eliminated 6,634 possibilities, refining and narrowing his search as he proceeded, drawing him closer and closer to his goal.

Two other failures you may have heard of are Levi Strauss and Christopher Columbus. Strauss headed for the gold mines of California in hopes of gold and glory. But he found neither. Instead, this failure gave him new knowledge of a gap in the marketplace. He began selling pants made out of denim for the miners who were succeeding. Today, we've all heard of Levi Strauss jeans. Columbus failed miserably to achieve his goal of finding a route to India. However, in failing he encountered a fresh opportunity—the New World. By taking action and learning from your mistakes and failures, you'll gain new knowledge and become aware of many new opportunities. When you come to the edge of what you know, it's time to make some mistakes.

> "When you come to the edge of what you know, it's time to make some mistakes."

Building Quality Relationships

In business and in life, it is what you know, who you know, *and* how well you know them that determines the opportunities you have and whether you can reach your goals. You must make an exerted effort to get out there and build relationships. Any single person you meet just might become your next business partner or largest client. Any single person you meet knows hundreds of other people to whom they can refer you, if you just take the time to establish a relationship. When I taught a group of high school students in the summer of 2003 in Boston and Chicago, I told them to think of every student at their school as a valuable person who could help them in many unforeseen ways 10, 20, or 70 years down the road. You must view everyone you meet in the same manner.

In every business I have ever had, the best advertising has been word of mouth and referrals from other customers. Humans are social creatures and will give much more credence to a referral than to an advertisement. You'll be amazed at the amount of business you can generate just by doing things like asking those you know about others who could use your products or services, joining your local Chamber of Commerce, or volunteering in your community. Here are a few more tips for networking:

- Never burn your bridges.
- Send thank-you cards.
- Have plenty of business cards on hand.
- Follow up when asked to do a favor for someone from whom you might need a favor down the line.
- Strategically volunteer with organizations that have members or directors you'd like to network with.
- Ask to shadow people whom you would like to get to know and whose job positions interest you.
- Connect those in your network who you think might be able to help each other.
- Invite those who have experience in business or your industry to serve on an informal advisory board for your company.

Action Item 7: Finding Mentors through Lunch Dates

Phase 1: Take a moment to write down the names of any people who have already done what you want to accomplish. If you don't know any specific individuals, write down the names of people who may be able to connect you to persons who have already done what you wish to accomplish.

_____

_____

_____

_____

Phase 2: Make a commitment to yourself to figure out how to contact these people and ask them to have lunch with you so that you can ask them a few questions about how to get started or improve your business.

I, _____, commit to asking each person on the preceding list to at least have lunch with me in the next six weeks.

Signed

X_____ Date: _____

You would be surprised how many people whom you thought were unreachable or unavailable are willing to meet you, if you ask authentically for help and have a flexible calendar.

Phase 3: Have lunch with the people who respond favorably and learn as much as you can. If you hit it off with any individual, ask the person if he or she would be willing to act as an informal mentor to you and meet with you every few months. Everyone you meet will likely be able to connect you to another individual who can help you. Send a thank-you card in return and let them know you very much appreciated their time and that you'd be happy to help them in any way you can.

Building a large and valuable network is not something that can be done in a few weeks. It takes years. I place great importance on my networks—both my local network and my worldwide network. Since age 17, when I realized the importance of building a network, I have carefully kept track of all those with whom I come in contact.

I use what I call a "top-of-the-funnel" strategy and add every person I meet to my contact database. I keep notes on the last time I spoke to them, the organizations with which they are affiliated, and any other pertinent information. I then keep in touch with all of these people, every so often e-mailing them updates on what I am up to as well as my Entrepreneurship Chronicle and Email Marketing Monthly newsletter.

I group my network by segments so I can send targeted information and leverage each segment when it is needed. Segments include my personal advisory board, friends and family, college entrepreneurs, book updates, press contacts, international entrepreneurs, people with whom I can stay when I go on a book tour, and the entrepreneurship newsletter recipients. It amazes me how much more value I get from my network by simply staying in touch.

As part of your networking effort, always be on the lookout for potential mentors. You'll find that a commonality among successful entrepreneurs is that, at some time or another, each had a mentor who was essential in getting them from one level to the next in business.

If there is someone you respect or someone who is in a position you'd like to be in someday, ask that person to lunch. The worst that could happen is that he or she will say no. If you do go to lunch, ask this person about the challenges he or she has faced in getting to his or her current position, and solicit the person's advice. If you've established rapport, ask the person to act as a formal mentor to you and set up a monthly lunch date.

In general, most people are willing to help you. You must ask, however, and you must be genuine about it. You must be willing to take a chance, take a risk, and ask someone. You must have confidence. You must not approach the person with a sales pitch, but rather with a few questions to elicit the person's advice.

If you can find a link between yourself and another person—such as the same alma mater or a common industry—the person is likely to be open to a phone call or exchange of e-mails with you. At the end of your meeting, always ask for referrals. You can achieve nearly any positive goal by asking for help and for referrals.

The Carolina Entrepreneurship Club at UNC runs two programs that are designed to help business owners build relationships. The first is called MentorMatch. This program matches successful entrepreneurs from the Raleigh, North Carolina, chapter of the Entrepreneurs' Organization with undergraduate student members of the club for a lunch. If the entrepreneur and student agree, they can establish a formal mentoring relationship after the first lunch, although neither is under any obligation.

The second program that has met with great success is the monthly Business Roundtable. All the members of the club who either own a business or are thinking about starting one are invited to these roundtables. At each meeting, participants talk about the progress they've made with their companies and any issues they are facing. The group has been a terrific learning experience for the newer members and a very helpful source of peer advice for the more experienced members. Classic personal development writer Napoleon Hill called such events "Mastermind Groups" and has emphasized their value throughout his work. Seek out similar MentorMatch programs or roundtables in your area.

No matter how you define success, no one can climb Mt. Everest, win an election, or build a million-dollar-business without the help of many people. Start building your network now and you'll reach your goals much faster.

A Note for Teenage Entrepreneurs from the Author

In case anyone reading this book is considering starting their own company instead of going to college, let me say this: Be very careful. I would say that both a college degree and the college experience are extremely beneficial for most people. College can be a great time to refine a business plan and build the contacts needed to make it a reality, so make your decision carefully. The value of friendships and alma mater connections and the additional experience of "learning how to learn" are undeniably valuable.

If you can work on your business while you are in college, you can create a tremendous foundation for your success after you graduate. My rule of thumb is this: if, before or during college, you can get a business started that makes more than $5,000 in sales per month, feel free to take time off to focus on the business. Until the business gets to that point, stay in school and work toward finishing.

If you do choose to start a business while you are in college or instead of college, make sure you have a mentor and a support team to help you along the way. The two young adults I know who have been able to create successful companies without going to college had mentors who helped them with their businesses; developed support teams of lawyers, CPAs, and boards of directors; and hired top-quality talent to help manage and grow their businesses. Furthermore, you need a good idea that can scale beyond being a local business. No matter how hard you work, if you cannot provide a service or product that the market demands, you will not succeed.

College is not a prerequisite for success in business by any means, but it can be a path. There are plenty of ways to network, develop as a person, and learn what you want to learn without being in a structured educational environment. However, if you have other goals such as becoming a teacher, scientist, engineer, or politician, or working in a large corporation, a degree is usually necessary.

Finally, I have seen many motivated people who did not go to college simply fall into idleness instead of building a support network and successful business. Do not let this happen to you. Whether you go to college or not, you have the potential to fulfill your dreams. Just keep at it and work hard.

The Power of Direction and Focus

Many people go through life without direction to guide them. They never set goals for themselves, or if they do, they fail to take any steps toward accomplishing those goals. If you are to become a successful entrepreneur, you must learn how to set goals and plan—for the short, mid-, and long term.

I definitely recommend that you cultivate a bias toward action, but you cannot know what action to take without planning. I use what I call the Outer-Dissection Method to set goals and plan the process necessary to achieve them. The name describes the overall strategy: start with your goals and then work backward to break everything down into smaller and smaller pieces and subgoals.

Establish your main, overall goal and from that, create particular strategies for accomplishing those goals. A strategy could take 1 year or 30 years to accomplish. A corporate planning sheet using this method might look like the one in Figure 13.1. A personal chart would resemble this, but it would omit the ownership category; you would be the owner of each step.

Within each strategy, create a series of tactics that, as a whole, allow you to accomplish the strategies. Each tactic might take as long as six months or as little as a few weeks. Finally, break these tactics into individual tasks. Within each tactic, there might be a handful or hundreds of individual tasks that must be accomplished. It is important that there be deadlines for each task, tactic, strategy, and goal.

As an example, your goal might be to win the Nobel Prize in Economics. One strategy for accomplishing this goal is to go to a top school to get your Ph.D. One tactic needed to accomplish this strategy would be to get good grades during your undergraduate education. One task to accomplish this tactic might be to do your homework tonight.

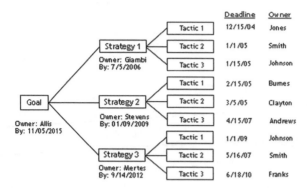

Figure 13.1 Tracking goals, strategies, tactics, deadlines, and accountability.

We are taking large goals and breaking them down into smaller and smaller subsections—and then working diligently on accomplishing each step. There is tremendous power in focusing on what you need to achieve in the short term (for me, finishing this chapter) and midterm (for me, building iContact) while being well aware of how these efforts integrate into your long-term plan (for me, working to improve the world on a global scale through entrepreneurship, social entrepreneurship, investing, politics, public policy, and philanthropy).

Becoming Driven and Passionate

The common denominator among every single highly driven and successful person I have ever met, regardless of field, is that they have committed their goals to writing and created for themselves a purpose-driven life. It is my belief that every passionate individual can benefit tremendously from creating a Personal Goals List, Chief Definite Purpose (I call this a BHALG, or big hairy audacious lifetime goal), and Personal Mission Statement, written down and posted where they sleep.

> A goal is a dream with a deadline.
>
> **—Napoleon Hill**

Below I share the three-phase process that I have developed (partially organically and partially with the guidance of the books *Think and Grow Rich, Good to Great, The Seven Habits of Highly Effective People, How to Win Friends and Influence People,* and *The*

Action Item 8: Create Your Personal Goals List

Phase 1: Find a quiet place and take some time to think about where your life is now and what your goals and plans are for the future. List your short-term (0 to 6 months), midterm (6 to 24 months), long-term (2 to 10 years), and then lifetime goals:

Short-Term Goals (0 to 6 Months)

_____

_____

_____

_____

_____

Midterm Goals (6 to 24 Months)

_____

_____

_____

_____

_____

_____

Long-Term Goals (2 to 10 Years)

_____

_____

_____

_____

_____

_____

Lifetime Goals (10+ Years)

_____

_____

_____

_____

_____

_____

Phase 2: Share your goals with people close to you whom you trust, and get feedback on how to go about accomplishing these goals. Speak with people who will build you up and support you in your efforts rather than telling you that you will never accomplish this dream. Type and print out your Personal Goals List, post it in your bedroom, then review it at least annually.

Secret) to help me become a driven, passionate individual who wakes up every day motivated to work toward my short-term, midterm, and long-term goals.

The next phase is to create at least one Big Hairy Audacious Lifetime Goal (BHALG). This can be your chief definite aim and part of your core purpose of being. You may or may not already have a BHALG. Regardless, thinking about it and committing it to writing

Action Item 9: Write Your BHALG

Phase 1: Take a moment and write down a Big Hairy Audacious Lifetime Goal (BHALG). If you do not already have a clear BHALG that comes to mind, make this goal something you believe is next to impossible, something that up until *right now*, you never thought you could or would actually have the ability to accomplish. This may take a few days or a few months to come up with, or it may flow naturally. Think big and think globally.

_____

_____

_____

Phase 2: Share your BHALG with people close to you whom you trust, and get feedback on how to go about accomplishing it. Speak with people who will build you up and support you in your efforts rather than telling you that you will never accomplish this dream. Type and print your BHALG, and tape it to the wall of your bedroom.

Phase 3: Dissect the strategies, tactics, and tasks that you will need to accomplish this goal, and go for it. Play life like a long-term game and create five-year game plans that build upon one another to allow you reach this goal within 30 years. While ensuring your own happiness, never forget your BHALG. If you know without a doubt that you will accomplish this goal, you will. If you don't think you will, you will not. Make it a driving chief definite purpose, while understanding the investments you need to make along the way to make it possible.

will give you a better chance of enduring whatever adversity you have to go through in your quest to achieve it.

Don't be afraid to set your goals high; often you'll learn new things and meet new people along the way that will allow you to accomplish things you might think impossible today. Furthermore, if you shoot for the stars, you'll land on the treetops—but if you shoot for the tree-tops, you'll land in a mud pit. Once you've detailed each of your goals, write a short, one-paragraph mission statement that summarizes your most important goals. My personal mission statement at age 18 was as follows:

> To be a founder or cofounder of a company with greater than $2 million in sales by age 21, to be financially free, to take a company public, to write a best-selling book, to be happy, to marry and have kids, and to set up a foundation to encourage education, reduce poverty, improve health, better economic conditions, encourage entrepreneurship, and prevent corruption in developing nations.

My personal mission statement at 23 is:

> To be one of the leaders of a generational movement to improve the United States and the world through entrepreneurship, social entrepreneurship, investing, public service, and philanthropy, thereby increasing access to opportunity and creating stronger global societies, while being financially free, taking multiple companies public, creating thousands of quality jobs, driving innovation, writing a best-selling book, being happy, marrying and having children, and setting up a foundation to work on reducing poverty, ensuring environmental sustainability, and investing in human understanding, education, health care, and microfinance.

Now, write your own Personal Mission Statement.

Now that you have a Personal Goals List, a BHALG, and a Personal Mission Statement and can see things on the macro scale, you

Action Item 10: Write Your Personal Mission Statement

Phase 1: Take a moment to write a draft of your Personal Mission Statement, including the major goals you have for your life.

_____

_____

_____

_____

_____

Phase 2: Type up your Personal Mission Statement, print it out, and tape it to the wall in your bedroom.

can begin the planning process that allows you to execute in the short term. To complete this part of the process, I do certain things weekly, monthly, and annually.

Every Sunday night I spend approximately three hours catching up on e-mails from the past week and planning out the next week. I send myself e-mails about any open tasks that I need to complete. About twice per week I write in a journal, reviewing the day, who I met, what I accomplished, any mistakes I made, and what is coming up. Finally, at least once per week I read both my Personal Prayer and the Entrepreneurs' Creed, framed versions of which I have both at home and in my office. Reading these inspires me and gives me the motivation I need to push through adversity and execute. Readers can create their own prayers and creeds based on their own faith.

The second part of this process is the monthly review. On the last day of each month, I review everything that I have accomplished each

Personal Prayer

God, thank you for my life. Thank you for all the blessings you have bestowed upon me and the gifts you have endowed me with. I pray this moment for those who are not as fortunate as I, those in need, and those under duress. I hope to have the wisdom and strength to dedicate my life as an entrepreneur, writer, investor, and politician to improving standards of living, removing corruption, bettering lives, and reducing hurt in my country and across our world. God, let me be strong and grant me wisdom to proceed on this venture. Grant me the ability to live my life to the fullest. Grant me the control to think accurately and master my mind, the will to be consistently unique, the ability to be a master of relations, the motivation to excel, and the energy, health, and enthusiasm to never waste a moment of your precious gift. God, thank you for my life.

The Entrepreneurs' Creed

I set myself before this world as an entrepreneur. I analyze the markets and take educated risks through planned ventures and investments. I accept the basic law of the entrepreneur—that of supply and demand. If I am right, I will be rewarded with capital and stature. If I am not, I will bankrupt my accounts, yet gain in wisdom so as to improve chances on my next try. While keeping in mind externalities, I create what we, as humans, demand, and in turn make the world an improved place for all. Through my work I help create dynamic economies in which the standard of living is always increasing through innovation and technological progress. Through my work I encourage competition and provide lower prices on and a higher quality and a better selection of goods and services. Toward this end I shall always be persistent, continually learn, be a master of relations, and be forever motivated to excel. I am an entrepreneur. Grant me strength, vision, persistence, motivation, and energy.

month, the new relationships I developed, the mistakes I made, and how I have progressed toward my goals. I reanalyze how I want to set my priorities going forward, and refocus on my goals. Here is a review of the planning processes I go through:

- *Weekly:* Write in your journal at least twice per week, covering who you met, what was accomplished, the mistakes made, and what is coming up. Read your personal prayer at least weekly. Catch up on your correspondence and plan out your week each Sunday night.
- *Monthly:* On the last day of each month, write a review of what you accomplished in the previous month along with how you are progressing toward your short- and midterm goals.
- *Annually:* During the last week of every year, read over all the monthly reviews and create a plan for the next year highlighting what you will be focusing on and what new strategies and tactics you should pursue. Set your annual goals and review your progress toward last year's goals. Also, read over your Personal Mission Statement and update it if need be.
- *Every five years:* Write a 20- to 25-page personal plan describing what you wish to accomplish over the upcoming four years. Sign this document and get feedback on it from close associates.

In my experience, there are six core steps in accomplishing any goal, including that of building a business. These are:

1. Write down goals.
2. Create a vision and a strategy.
3. Implement actions.
4. Measure results and obtain feedback.
5. Find what works and make a midcourse correction.
6. Repeat the process, building upon your successes and learning from your mistakes.

This process, repeated continuously, will guide you toward accomplishing any goal. While using it will not guarantee success, as

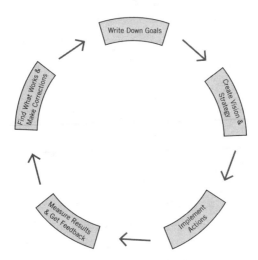

Figure 13.2 The cycle of setting and achieving larger and larger goals.

this is based on the strength of the strategy and numerous other ex-ogenous variables, this model can be of great help in structuring your progress and refining your plan. As Napoleon Hill says, "If you can conceive it and you can believe it you can achieve whatever you set your sights on."

It is absolutely amazing what life can bring and what the universe can provide if you simply go through the process of identifying what you truly want out of life and then focusing on making that desire a reality.

Becoming Great

In this world, each of us has the opportunity to be either great or mediocre. Presuming you've determined that you want to become great yourself, it helps to see the other traits that great people have in common. Here are some of the characteristics that enable great people to come up with and develop world-changing ideas:

- Ability to communicate
- Ability to judge

- Ability to motivate
- Adaptability
- Courage
- Curiosity
- Devotion to goals
- Drive
- Dynamic energy
- Enterprise
- Enthusiasm
- Honesty
- Idealism
- Imagination
- Individualism
- Knowledge
- Optimism
- Outgoingness
- Patience
- Perception
- Persuasion
- Sales ability
- Sense of humor
- Versatility
- Willingness to take risks

Giving Back

When I was 20 years old, I performed an exercise that changed my life forever. I wrote down how I wanted to use my life to make a difference in the world—to help build stronger communities and societies here at home, and also to work to end poverty and hunger globally. When I learned from reading an annual report from the World Health Organization that over 18 million people die every year (49,365 per day) from preventable diseases and starvation, the gravity of some of the most important issues of our day hit me.

When I learned from a World Bank report that as of 2001, 2.7 billion people live on under $2 per day (42 percent of the humans in the world), the realization made me want to spend my life working entrepreneurially to address these issues. When I read *The End of Poverty* (Penguin, 2006), by Columbia University economist Jeffrey Sachs in 2006, I further committed to being a leader of my generation to address the problems and ensuring that by the end of my life at least 95 percent of the wealth I generate goes back to creating societies with greater access to opportunity and sustainably assisting people who have not had the opportunity I have been so fortunate to have.

As I added to my knowledge through travel, reading, and speaking with people who live in developing nations, I updated my Mission Statement and began to write what I call a Purpose Statement. Along the way, the added depth of purpose has given what I strive to do every day deep personal meaning. For me, entrepreneurship is not about making lots of money and living an extravagant life; it's about being able to make a positive impact in the lives of thousands and, hopefully someday, billions. Discovering how starting and building a successful business can bring a larger meaning into your life and allow you to give back to your community, you will be able to more easily find your core motivation and align what you do with what you love.

Finding a deeper meaning and core motivation for doing what you do is a critically important part of getting through the difficult times along the way to becoming a successful businessperson. I have found this meaning for myself. Here is my Purpose Statement:

> I wish to spend my life working through entrepreneurship, social entrepreneurship, investing, philanthropy, public policy, and politics to end poverty in developing nations and at home, ensure environmental sustainability, help people understand that we are one humanity and that our commonalities are much greater than our differences, and help expand access to opportunity, health care, and education across the world for every human of every nation.

Right now, write down how you hope to use your talents, resources, and time on this planet to make a positive difference in the world. This can be a powerful exercise, so please take some time to complete it.

Action Item 11: Finding Deeper Purpose in Your Life

Take some time to write how you hope to use your business, time, energy, and resources to make a positive difference in the world.

I wish to spend my life . . .

_____

_____

_____

_____

_____

_____

_____

_____

_____

_____

_____

Many extremely successful industrialists and entrepreneurs over the past 150 years have chosen to give back. Andrew Carnegie funded libraries all over the United States and created his foundation to "promote the advancement and diffusion of knowledge and understanding." John D. Rockefeller created the Rockefeller Foundation to "promote the well-being of mankind throughout the world." Henry Ford created the Ford Foundation to "promote democracy, reduce poverty, promote international understanding, and advance human achievement." Bill Gates has created the Bill and Melinda Gates Foundation to "enhance global healthcare and reduce global poverty and expand access to educational opportunity and technology." Gates has said many times that he will give 95 percent of his wealth back to society before he dies. He considers himself a steward of wealth, as should any successful entrepreneur.

For entrepreneurs, the score is kept on the basis of who can create the most value. Money comes to you in direct proportion to how much value you create by rearranging the resources of land, labor, capital, and entrepreneurial ability into the outputs that society desires. If we are successful, we can create millions, perhaps billions, of dollars of value for society and in turn become wealthy through stock appreciation, going public, or selling the company.

I hope you will give back what you can along the way as you build your company—and especially after you have become wealthy. It is our job as enlightened entrepreneurs to give back to the society and the world that have enabled us to succeed, to work to create fuller access to opportunity. Giving back can bring a wealth of meaning and purpose to our lives, and make us more driven entrepreneurs at the same time.

Action Item 12:
The Enlightened Entrepreneur's Commitment

I, _____ _____, commit to contributing at least 90 percent of any wealth I earn during my lifetime to a personal foundation or endowments of charitable organizations that will work to address the major issues of our world such as poverty, hunger, education, health care, environmental sustainability, and any other area that I believe will make the world, my nation, my state, and my community a better place.

X_____ Date: _____

4. If you presently do not have the financial resources, the experience, or a good business idea, intern or get a job at a company in an industry you are interested in and start building your network and gaining experience.
5. Always focus on building quality relationships with good people.
6. Regardless of what you are doing, make sure you are constantly learning.
7. Take a proactive role in planning, goal setting, and personal evaluation.
8. Don't be afraid to ask for help. People are often very willing to help you if you ask genuinely.
9. Get experience however you can, build your network, have confidence, and be in it to win. It is up to you. Get out there and do it. Take the initiative and have a bias toward action.
10. If and when you succeed, give back. There are so many brothers and sisters in our world who are not as fortunate as you and I have been.

Good luck as you build your business and progress in your life. Do let me know if I can be of assistance to you in your journey (my e-mail address is ryan@icontact.com). Know that how you go about your journey is just as important as what you do once you've reached your destination. If I can inspire just one person who ends up making a positive difference in the world and helps others do the same, my job will be done. I hope that person is you.

APPENDIXES

Appendix 1:
FINANCIAL VOCABULARY

Building your financial intelligence is a key task along the path toward becoming a successful entrepreneur. Following is a list of financial vocabulary terms with easy-to-understand definitions. This list includes common accounting, investing, and business terms.

Accounts Payable: Money you owe for products and services already received.

Accounts Receivable: Money owed to you for products and services already delivered.

Angel Investor: A private high-net-worth individual who will invest money in medium- or high-potential ventures in exchange for a percentage of ownership in a company.

Appreciating Asset: Something you own that is going up in value.

Appreciation: An increase in value over time.

Asset: Something you own that has value.

Balance Sheet Formula: Assets minus liabilities equals owners' equity (A – L = OE).

Balance Sheet: A financial statement that keeps track of assets, liabilities, and owners' equity.

Bond: A debt instrument through which companies and governments can raise money.

Cash Flow: The in and out of money to and from your business.

Cash Flow Statement: A financial statement that keeps track of all the money that goes in and out of your business.

COGS: The cost of goods sold. What you pay for what you sell.

Depreciating Asset: Something you own that is going down in value.

Depreciation: A reduction in value over time.

EBITDA: Earnings before interest, taxes, depreciation, and amortization.

Equity: Ownership in a company.

Expenses: What you spend.

Gross Income: Total revenue minus COGS.

Gross Margin: The same as *gross income*.

Income Statement: A financial statement that keeps track of revenue, expenses, and profit.

Income Statement Formula: Revenue minus expenses equals net income (R − E = NI).

IPO: Initial public offering, selling part of your company on the stock market in exchange for investment capital in your business.

Liability: Something you owe, or something that is taking money out of your pocket each month with no positive cash return.

Net Income: The same as *net profit*.

Net Profit: Total revenue minus total expenses.

Option Pool: A percentage of ownership in your company set aside at founding for those who may come on board later.

Owners' Equity: The value of what the shareholders/owners have put into a company.

Revenue: What you earn.

Venture Capital: Investment money raised from firms that invest in high-potential ventures in exchange for a percentage of ownership in a company.

Vesting: Earning equity over time instead of all at once.

Appendix 2:
RECOMMENDED BOOKS

The following books were consulted in writing *Zero to One Million* and are recommended for further reading.

Globalization and Economics

Ball, Terence, and Richard Dagger. *Political Ideologies and the Democratic Ideal*. Longman, 2005.

DeSoto, Hernando. *The Mystery of Capital: Why Capitalism Triumphs in the West and Fails Everywhere Else*. Basic Books, 2000.

Friedman, Thomas L. *The Lexus and the Olive Tree: Understanding Globalization*. Anchor Books, 2000.

———. *The World Is Flat: A History of the Twenty-first Century*. Farrar, Straus and Giroux, 2005.

Heilbroner, Robert L. *The Worldly Philosophers: The Lives, Times and Ideas of the Great Economic Thinkers*. Touchstone, 1999.

McMillan, John. *Reinventing the Bazaar: A Natural History of Markets*. Norton, 2003.

Perkins, John. *The Secret History of the American Empire: Economic Hit Men, Jackals, and the Truth about Global Corruption*. Dutton Adult, 2007.

Stiglitz, Joseph. *Globalization and Its Discontents*. Norton, 2002.

Yergin, Daniel, and Joseph Stanislaw. *The Commanding Heights: the Battle Between Government and the Marketplace That Is Remaking the Modern World.* Simon & Schuster, 1998.

Entrepreneurship

Allen, Robert G. *Multiple Streams of Income: How to Generate a Lifetime of Unlimited Wealth.* Wiley, 2000.

Allis, Ryan P. M. *Zero to One Million: How to Build a Company to $1 Million in Sales.* Virante, 2003.

Burns, Tim. *Entrepreneurship.com.* Upstart Publishing, 2000.

Kiyosaki, Robert T. *Rich Dad Poor Dad.* Time Warner, 2002.

Kiyosaki, Robert T., and Sharon Lechter. *Rich Dad's Guide to Investing: What the Rich Invest In, That the Poor and the Middle Class Do Not!* Business Plus, 2000.

Kushell, Jennifer. *The Young Entrepreneurs' Edge: Using Your Ambition, Independence, and Youth to Launch a Successful Business.* Princeton Review, 1999.

Mariotti, Steve. *The Young Entrepreneur's Guide to Starting and Running a Business.* Three Rivers, 2000.

Timmons, Jeffrey. *New Venture Creation: Entrepreneurship in the 21st Century.* McGraw-Hill, 1995.

Marketing

Gladwell, Malcolm. *Blink: The Power of Thinking Without Thinking.* Little, Brown, 2005.

————. *The Tipping Point: How Little Things Can Make a Big Difference.* Little, Brown, 2000.

Godin, Seth. *Permission Marketing: Turning Strangers into Friends, and Friends into Customers.* Simon & Schuster, 1999.

————. *Purple Cow: Transform Your Business by Being Remarkable.* Portfolio, 2003.

————. *Unleashing the Ideavirus.* Hyperion, 2001.

Levinson, Jay Conrad. *Guerrilla Marketing: Secrets for Making Big Profits from Your Small Business.* Houghton Mifflin, 1998.

Rosen, Emanuel. *The Anatomy of Buzz: Creating Word of Mouth Marketing.* HarperCollins, 2000.

Management

Bossidy, Larry. *Execution: The Discipline of Getting Things Done.* Crown Business, 2002.

Collins, Jim. *Good to Great: Why Some Companies Make the Leap . . . and Others Don't.* Collins, 2001.

Collins, Jim, and Jerry I. Porras. *Built to Last: Successful Habits of Visionary Companies.* HarperBusiness, 1994.

Fick, Nathaniel. *One Bullet Away.* Weidenfeld & Nicolson, 2006.

Welch, Jack. *Winning.* HarperBusiness, 2005.

Personal Development

Byrne, Rhonda. *The Secret.* Atria, 2006.

Carnegie, Dale. *How to Win Friends and Influence People.* Vermilion, 2007.

Covey, Steven R. *The Seven Habits of Highly Effective People.* Free Press, 1989.

Hill, Napoleon. *The Law of Success in Sixteen Lessons.* HN Publishing, 2006.

———. *Succeed and Grow Rich Through Persuasion.* Signet, 1989.

———. *Think and Grow Rich.* Aventine, 2004.

Kushell, Jennifer, with Scott M. Kaufman. *Secrets of the Young & Successful: How to Get Everything You Want Without Waiting a Lifetime.* Fireside, 2003.

Robbins, Anthony. *Unlimited Power: The New Science of Perosnal Achievement.* Free Press, 1997.

Simmons, Michael. *The Student Success Manifesto: How to Create a Life of Passion, Purpose, and Prosperity.* Extreme Entrepreneurship Education Co., 2003.

Stanley, Thomas J., Ph.D. *The Millionaire Mind.* Andrews McMeel, 2000.

Appendix 3:
RESOURCES FOR ENTREPRENEURS

Here is a list of a few resources and organizations that may be of help to you along your entrepreneurial journey.

- Allbusiness Small Business Resource (www.allbusiness.com). Top resource for small to midsize business owners and entrepreneurs.
- Collegiate Entrepreneurs Organization (www.c-e-o.org). Organization for undergraduate students interested in entrepreneurship.
- Entrepreneur Magazine Online–(www.entrepreneur.com). Magazine content, resources, and community for entrepreneurs and business owners.
- Entrepreneurs' Organization (www.eonetwork.org). Worldwide under-40 organization for entrepreneurs with businesses with revenues U.S. $1 million+ yearly.
- EntreWorld–(www.entreworld.com). Articles and content for entrepreneurs.
- Ewing Marion Kauffman Foundation–(www.emkf.org). Foundation encouraging and supporting entrepreneurship.
- Inc. Magazine Online.–(www.inc.com. Magazine content,

resources, and community for entrepreneurs and business owners.

- Junior Achievement (www.ja.org). Organization that promotes the free enterprise system through volunteers and classroom-based interactive learning.
- Let's Talk Business Network–(www.ltbn.com). Syndicated radio show on business and entrepreneurship.
- National Commission on Entrepreneurship–(www.ncoe.org). Active entrepreneurship policy group on Capitol Hill sponsored by the Kauffman Foundation.
- Service Corps of Retired Executives–(www.score.org). Have your questions answered by experienced business professionals.
- Start-Up Nation–(www.startupnation.com). Great start-up resource from the acclaimed Sloan Brothers.
- Students in Free Enterprise (www.sife.org). Organizes university competition for completing projects related to free enterprise.
- The Lowe Foundation–(www.lowe.org). Foundation supporting the entrepreneurial spirit.
- Young and Successful (www.youngandsuccessful.com). Content for entrepreneurs and database of thousands of entrepreneurs worldwide.
- YoungEntrepreneur.com–(www.youngentreprenuer.com). Articles and information for entrepreneurs ages 0 to 40 and small business owners.
- Zeromillion.com (www.zeromillion.com). Companion site to this book, containing over 3,000 articles on entrepreneurship, business, economics, personal development, marketing, and Web marketing; interviews with entrepreneurs; and a discussion forum.

Appendix 4:

THE MISSION OF THE HUMANITY CAMPAIGN

Throughout this book, I have mentioned the nonprofit organization that I have founded and the goals that I have for it. Here is a bit of additional information on our mission and purpose.

The Humanity Campaign was founded in November 2005. It is based in Chapel Hill, North Carolina. Our mission is to increase access to education, health care, and technology, reduce poverty and hunger, ensure environmental sustainability, and encourage the realization among world leaders that we are all part of one humanity and that we have more in common than what separates us.

Our strategy for accomplishing this goal is to make entrepreneurship and business development possible for every person in every country, fight corrupt government and business, work with governmental and nongovernmental organizations to enhance the business and social infrastructure, establish proper legal and property ownership systems, promote free trade and remove tariffs and subsidies, improve entrepreneurship and business education at the grassroots level in every country, and connect entrepreneurs, investors, and governments at every level so as to encourage the exchange of contacts, ideas, methods, and investment capital.

We believe that competitive market economies, free from collusion and corruption, are essential to creating an incentive to produce and thus are essential to a high standard of living. We believe that the ability to be an entrepreneur should be made available to every human from every country. To this end, we will promote efficient competitive market economies that take into account those at both ends of the socioeconomic ladder.

We believe in promoting the principles of liberalism. We believe in a republic and democratic system of government, religious freedom, and the promotion of individual initiative. We believe there is a distinct and important role, though limited, for government, especially in the early stages of a country's development.

We want to give the more than 2 billion persons who live on under $1 per day the chance and ability to make something of themselves, create a life free of poverty, and provide value to society. Presently, breaking out of poverty, becoming an entrepreneur, or significantly improving one's status is not possible for the majority of people in the world. In the way are corruption in government and deficiencies in business and social infrastructure, proper legal frameworks, entrepreneurship education for those at the lower socioeconomic end of society, and communication among aspiring entrepreneurs.

To reach this goal we will follow the tactics given in our strategy stated above. We will

1. Encourage and teach entrepreneurship in every country
2. Fight political and business corruption
3. Help build the business and social infrastructure
4. Lobby against protectionism and the removal of subsidies and tariffs
5. Help establish proper legal and property ownership systems
6. Connect entrepreneurs at all levels with investors and governments

First, we will encourage entrepreneurship at every level. The skills of always improving processes, focusing on efficiency, and properly managing people will be important to all members of society. While not everyone will want to be an entrepreneur, we believe that it is a right of mankind to be able to start a business, create value, and, if a business succeeds, profit from working hard and intelligently.

We must democratize entrepreneurship and streamline governmental systems so as to create a society in which it is not just those with money and connections who are able to start a business. We believe that entrepreneurship creates competition in the marketplace, creates an efficient use of resources and distribution of goods and services for society's needs, and over time ensures that the price of goods and services goes down while the quality goes up—thus increasing standards of living.

We must teach entrepreneurship in the villages, towns, and cities, and in the schools and homes. Often this will not be the type of entrepreneurship you'd learn in American business schools. There will often be no venture capital, no down-rounds, no initial public offerings, no option pools, and no seasoned executives to attract. Rather, we'll just as often be teaching how to register a business in a country, the difference between a balance sheet and an income statement, or the difference between revenue and profit. We hope to be at all levels, from working with governments and NGOs such as the World Trade Organization and World Bank to arranging methods of international distribution and trade for local artisans and farmers to helping write the curriculum at a new graduate business school in Nairobi to assisting with the creation of the first formal stock market in a country.

Crucial to our ability to reach our objectives will be the extent to which we are able to reduce political and business corruption in our world. While the majority of this has been routed out in developed countries over the past century, much still remains in developing nations. We must promote democratic elections, checks and balances in government, and the development of organizations that play roles similar to that of the Securities and Exchange Commission of the United States. We must fight despotism, nepotism, favoritism, fraud, tax evasion, and financial manipulation.

The third part of our strategy is to assist in the development of the business and social infrastructure. There are very few entrepreneurial support organizations, effective Chambers of Commerce, or universities completing top-tier research in developing countries. We must work to encourage the growth and assist in creating the structure for such organizations.

We must help to launch research labs, entrepreneurship clubs, and tech transfer offices at universities, encourage an active Chamber of Commerce in every sizable town, and bring entrepreneurial networking organizations such as the Entrepreneurs' Organization (EO), World Entrepreneurs' Organization (WEO), Service Corps of Retired Executives (SCORE), Collegiate Entrepreneurs' Organization (CEO), and The Indus Entrepreneurs (TiE) to the developing world. Finally, we will work to establish efficient tax systems and with part of this revenue, along with revenue from international aid, create a social safety net that gives a handout for a limited time and forever a hand up.

One of the major problems in our world today is that countries continue to have tariffs on foreign goods and subsidies for their domestic producers, hurting the people of other countries as well as their own countries. Through the General Agreement on Tariffs and Trade (GATT) and now the World Trade Organization (WTO), much progress has been made on this front since World War II.

While trade benefits us all, it can hurt specific segments of the population in the short term. We must make sure we help those who are negatively affected by trade in the short term with job retraining, educational grants, and assistance programs. We must also ensure the labor standards of our trading partners do not violate human rights guidelines.

As Peruvian economist Hernando de Soto notes in *The Other Path* and *The Mystery of Capital,* a significant problem in the developing world is the lack of formal property laws. Without official title to their land, even if it is only a 10-foot by 10-foot slum, the poor have little incentive to improve their house and surroundings and, just as important, they are unable to leverage this asset to obtain a microloan from the bank that they could use to start a small business or turn their wood panel or hardened mud walls into concrete or brick. We must establish formal property laws throughout developing nations and we must do this immediately. Further, we must establish legal systems that do not unduly benefit any party or caste, are fair to all members of a country, and take atrocities such as corruption and torture very seriously.

It will take many decades to build the Humanity Campaign into the foundation we hope it will become. There are many people who have dedicated their lives to increasing standards of living, solving the global problem of poverty, and encouraging economic development in the third world. We are with you and we hope you will be with us. For more information on our mission and organization, you can visit www.humanitycampaign.org and our topic-specific site on poverty at www.antipovertycampaign.org. If you might be interested in helping us achieve our goals, I encourage you to contact me at ryan@icontact.com.

Appendix 5:
JOIN THE COMMUNITY AT ZEROMILLION.COM

In July 2002, I decided to start an online entrepreneurship resource through which I could begin to develop a community. I registered the domain name www.zeromillion.com and began work on the Web site. I found a few friends to help me, and by the end of August, we had published over 150 articles on the topics of business, marketing, Web marketing, e-business entrepreneurship, young entrepreneurship, personal development, and economics.

Today, the site contains over 3,000 pages and features a lively discussion forum, dozens of interviews with CEOs and entrepreneurs, free e-books on Web marketing, an online journal of my adventures as a young entrepreneur, and the monthly Entrepreneurship Chronicle. I would encourage you to visit the site and join our community.

Whether you have questions on search engine optimization, want to discuss the latest about Web 2.0 or the UN's actions, or are looking to get feedback on your business idea, the discussion forums and content-rich sections of the site are a tremendous resource. You can join the community now at www.zeromillion.com/talk/.

I hope you will follow my journey as I work to build iContact. You can follow along through my blog at www.ryanallis.com/blog/ and friend me on Facebook. I thank you for reading *Zero to One Million* and hope you will recommend it to your friends and colleagues.

Yours entrepreneurially,
Ryan P.M. Allis

INDEX